WATER AND SPIRIT

ADRIENNE VON SPEYR

WATER AND SPIRIT

*Meditations on Saint John's Gospel
1:19—5:47*

Translated by
Sr. Lucia Wiedenhöver, O.C.D.

IGNATIUS PRESS   SAN FRANCISCO

Title of the German original:
Das Wort wird Fleisch
Betrachtungen über das Johannesevangelium, Kapitel 1–5
© 1949 Johannes Verlag, Einsiedeln
Published with ecclesiastical approval

Unless otherwise indicated, Scripture quotations
are from Revised Standard Version of the Bible—
Second Catholic Edition (Ignatius Edition) copyright
© 2006 National Council of the Churches of Christ
in the United States of America. Used by permission.
All rights reserved worldwide.

Cover art:
Saint John, Evangelist
Byzantine miniature, 12th century
Biblioteca Marciana, Venice, Italy
© Scala/Art Resource, New York

Cover design by Roxanne Mei Lum

© 2019 by Ignatius Press, San Francisco
All rights reserved
ISBN 978-1-62164-273-2
Library of Congress Control Number 2019931438
Printed in the United States of America ∞

CONTENTS

The Baptist's Witness	7
The Call of the Disciples	23
The Marriage at Cana	40
The Cleansing of the Temple	53
Nicodemus	67
The Friend of the Bridegroom	92
The Samaritan Woman	109
The Royal Official	154
The Sick Man at Bethesda	159
The Conferring of Judgment	169
The Testimony	202

THE BAPTIST'S WITNESS

1:19. *And this is the testimony of John, when the Jews sent priests and Levites from Jerusalem to ask him, "Who are you?"*
What the Jews are expecting is a grand, unambiguous answer; they are looking for something unexpected but at the same time clear-cut, valid once and for all, something satisfying that would reassure them and put an end to the matter. What they are in no way looking for is an answer exceeding the question and containing more than the question has asked; to expect this would mean an openness to faith, a possibility of being won over. The question would in a certain sense become a Christian one, if not with regard to its content, at least according to its spirit and disposition. But that is not how they ask. They do ask, however, and are so avid for an answer that they drop their human misgivings. They are clever enough to know exactly that the answer that now comes will be a real answer. But because they do not know Christ, they presume they are dealing with something that can be settled on the spot once and for all.

1:20. *He confessed, he did not deny, but confessed, "I am not the Christ."*
The first answer is: *I am not the Christ*. In order to give this answer, John must know very clearly who Christ is. Because he knows it so definitely, he knows with equal clarity who is not the Christ. The unambiguity of the response is founded on Christ and comes from him; it

is not clear who the one is who is not the Christ. He is one of the great number of men who are not Christ and have no possibility of being Christ. The Jews take it for granted that someone can be the Christ: John or someone else. It is merely a question of finding out who it is. They are disquieted; their disquiet resembles that of the disciples at the Last Supper. They know that one of them will betray, but they do not know who he is. In a similar way, the Jews know that somebody will now declare: I am the Christ. They know very well that the Christ is somewhere and that someone will now come forward to declare himself. They know: we shall meet him, which in no way means that we shall accept him and love him, but we shall know that he is the one. Two statements meet. On the one hand: we shall know who the Christ is. And on the other hand: *I am not the Christ.*

The Jews proceed from the sure characteristic of Christ, which is that he is the Christ. They know about the uniqueness of Christ but do not have the capacity to recognize him. John's capacity to recognize Christ rests on the fact that he knows: *I am not the Christ.* John knows of the distinctive mark of Christ that he has not got it himself. That is the full answer John gives, and he is not inclined at the moment to give another definition of himself. Thus, he is the man of truth. For him to recognize Christ means distinguishing himself from him. The others are blind; they are darkness. They grope their way to Christ in some manner; they have an indirect knowledge, an instinct that Christ is standing here somewhere; they grope for him as a blind man gropes for a color when he has been told that it lies in front of him. They feel that they will meet Christ. But they are not in love, and so they have to admit to their poverty of being obliged to ask at all. They are lacking in any gift of discernment because the discernment of spirits takes place only in love. Only within what is Christian can this discernment be made. Only here a Thou is no longer alone with another Thou; there is a communion in the Lord, in whose love one soul can embrace another one and slowly come to understand it in an empathy that is not merely human and psychological but also in an absolute immediate Christian experience, an experience of love, the only true and possible love, love in the Lord. The discernment of spirits in another person is rooted in the loving discernment of the Lord. John's love is discretion itself: it makes a distinction between itself and the Lord. John knows that anything that he can say positively about himself would entirely weaken his answer. It is a question, not of qualities, but of a Yes or No. In the negative answer, the others become aware of something in John that escapes them. His negative answer disquiets them still more; they recognize from it that he knows more than they do, that he even knows who the Christ is, which is something they do not know. This is the disquiet of those who know only that somewhere lies salvation but do not know where. And so they are dependent on the witness of others. They have set foot in a kingdom unknown to them, the kingdom of love. They do not know the rules of the game that are in force here. That does not make them guilty, but neither are they free to go on doing what they like. For at the moment the Lord appears, everyone is obliged to recognize him. This first meeting (before any meeting in reality) is the beginning itself; it is in every way the inchoative. It precedes any decision, but it is already seen in what direction the decision will be made. The inquirers should be in the state of openness, but they are not ready for this. They belong to those who are not of bad will; they sense that a demand will be made on them that they are not able to fulfill because they do not understand. Already in their first question, they miss the way because they think that they can come to a clarification and recognition in the normal way of asking questions. They make objective inquiries and do not know that they are already standing beyond the law of rational fact-finding. The familiar means of inquiry are already useless from the outset. They have missed the right route of access already at the first chance of an openness to Christianity. Had they received baptism, everything would be different; love would have been present from the beginning. But this foundation has not been laid in them. They are somehow to be pitied; they are the first of those of whom Christianity demands too much. At this moment, they are missing out on the usual Jewish lead, but they defend themselves as best they can. Recognizing in John something that has remained closed to them so far, they try, not without honesty, to disentangle the unfamiliar threads.

1:21. *And they asked him, "What then? Are you Elijah?" He said, "I am not." "Are you the prophet?" And he answered, "No."*

They know that John has some kind of a mission. So they go on asking, *"Are you Elijah?"* The first question was honest. The second already has an undertone of mockery. They feel reassured in some way, for they really know already that he is not Elijah. They feel somewhat superior again. But by feeling sure again that he is not Christ, they exchange a genuine disquiet for a false one; they turn it into a false disquiet that degenerates into a derisive benevolence. John again replies, *"I am not."* His second reply is now only a shadow of the first one, because he is now slowly forced to speak of himself and to say who he is, and this really is of no importance to him at all. His full answer has been given once and for all in his first one. The second question concerned himself, no longer the Lord. *"Are you the prophet?" He answered, "No."* Before the first question, it was said: *he did not deny, but confessed.* The second answer was *"I am not."* The third answer simply says, *"No."* His sentences become shorter. But the questions of the others are getting longer; they try to give an increasing weight to their question. As far as John is concerned, they are turning farther away from the main issue the more they turn to him, but to them it looks as if questioning in circles will lead to the real point.

1:22–23. *They said to him then, "Who are you? Let us have an answer for those who sent us. What do you say about yourself?" He said, "I am the voice of one crying in the wilderness, 'Make straight the way of the Lord,' as the prophet Isaiah said."*

In his positive answer, John says, not who he is, but what he is. He declares by this what the meaning of his being Christian is: it is to be an instrument. One can be foot, and another hand. He is *voice*. And not even the voice of the Lord, but only the voice of one who cries in the wilderness. I am not even part of the Lord, not a visible instrument, either, but something so unimportant that it has no substance. Only a voice, only the sound of an instrument, something passing, something that really does not exist at all. I am transitory. You want to hold me, you seek for me, but you can neither take hold of me nor grasp me, for I am only a voice. *Make straight the way of the Lord.* It does not even say, "Prepare the way." This is little, almost nothing. No real help, just a very small assistance. As he is a voice, something quite secondary, his effect will be only to facilitate things a bit. Nothing is said about the amount of facilitation. The way is already there, marked and measured, every curve of it. John comes only to make it easier.

He is only the suggestion of a help on the way, the mere outline of help. Here the role of every man in relation to the Lord is outlined, a double aspect of it. It is first made clear that man should give help toward Christ; this is his calling. Second, he must be on the way in order to be able to make it straight. This means that only what is on the way is of help and assistance to the Lord. Thus, the apparent help of those who want to help the Church without themselves believing is no real assistance, whether it comes from the state or from individuals. This kind of assistance can be transformed into real help only when it is used and passed on by believers themselves. With the help of unbelievers, the Lord cannot build anything. The unbeliever could not appeal to such help as a good work done to the Lord on the Day of Judgment. His work carries no weight. This is true in spite of the Lord's word about the glass of water that will not lose its reward and in spite of the promise that he will accept and count every act of love of neighbor as love shown to himself. For the love of neighbor of which the Lord speaks is always already a beginning of divine love, even outside the Church; it is always done to the Lord already suspected, not experienced. The help of unbelievers, however, is an insurance against love.

The way of the Lord. The questioners understand who is meant. They hear it. And because they hear and understand with the intellect what is meant, they also understand intellectually that Christ is the Lord. They grasp it as one grasps a historical fact. They are already now in possession of what will be their attitude in all that is to come to pass: a sense for right and justice. They know that John is right and gives right and just answers. They put the right questions to him and objectively understand what he is talking about. But they do not have love, and without love, there is no way to faith. The Pharisees do not love because they see and do not see. They see the picture, but with only one eye, without background, without depth, and one-dimensionally. It is love that gives life to faith and gives it the movement toward God, that makes it enthralling and contagious. Without love, faith is only an opinion, a theoretical insight, the adherence to a sentence. Love transforms it into a movement toward someone, faith in someone, reliance on someone. Christian faith never comes to birth without love. Love is the true school of faith. That is why loving trust in a human being, even erotic love, can become a *way* to faith in God; in this school, the spirit expands to be able to accept everything the beloved can give, even if it goes beyond one's own insight. This trust is lacking to the questioning Jews; it is lacking because the Holy Spirit is lacking to their faith, because it is the Holy Spirit alone who can enlarge human faith to the dimensions of God's infinity.

1:24–25. *Now they had been sent from the Pharisees. They asked him, "Then why are you baptizing, if you are neither the Christ, nor Elijah, nor the prophet?"*

They are open to the answer he gives about himself, without penetrating farther into it because they are without faith. Yet they take in the meaning of the words. They understand that his answer is absolute truth for him. They ask once more. They ask to complete their justice. They do not want to omit anything that could help to clarify the situation. Why does he baptize if he is not Christ or Elijah or the prophet? They understand this sequence in ascending order, while John hears it as descending. Because they do not understand in faith, the prophet is more to them than Elijah and Christ; they are more open to the sensation contained in the prophecy than to Christ; it is more real to them. But if they were to find a logical way that would lead them through a number of prophecies and proofs from the prophet to Christ, they would intellectually be ready to go this way.

1:26–28. *John answered them, "I baptize with water; but among you stands one whom you do not know, even he who comes after me, the thong of whose sandal I am not worthy to untie." This took place in Bethany beyond the Jordan, where John was baptizing.*

John responds, *"I baptize with water."* He does not answer their question at all, but still he endeavors to give a right answer. However, he already knows that they will not understand. He tries to lead them a step farther: he makes his own activity appear as unimportant as he himself sees it in order to point to the one who as the unknown *stands among them*. He does not give a description of him. He gives no indication of how he can be recognized. He knows that they do not know him and will not know him later, either; therefore, he does not try to make it more plausible to them. He simply states, *"You do not know ... he ... comes after me, the thong of whose sandal I am not worthy to untie."* That he comes after John means to the Pharisees that he is less important than the one who precedes him. This proves that they do not know him. John could have given some description; he could have said: I am not worthy to be compared with him; he could have given an idea of his spiritual and superior qualities. But he speaks only of the thong of his sandal, of something that is not essential to the Lord but related to him only externally. He knows that no description of the friend could bring him near to those who do not love. That is the reason why his own love speaks of the Lord with infinite tactfulness. While making him known, he protects him by his words and does not expose him; he does not hand over the intimacy of love to these outsiders. He reveals the friend by concealing him. But he does reveal him all the same by placing himself at an absolute distance from the Lord, by not in any way claiming intimacy with him and not ingratiating himself into the love of the Lord. Henceforth, Christian love will always be like this, in marriage, in friendship, in religious life, in any community. The unsaid is not always the unrevealed. There is a revelation through silence, as there is a silence for the sake of revelation. The Church's activity contains much revelation that is not expressed in words; every revelation begins with a word, but then one is drawn into its depth, and what is far greater begins to exercise its effect in silence.

All this happens *beyond the Jordan*, where the baptizing takes place. The whole conversation occurs in the face of this streaming water, which is a symbol of grace. For John baptizes the people in this stream to convey to them an image of the streams of grace that are to come, and the one they do not know is already standing among them; he will transform the symbol of water into the reality of the Spirit. The river Jordan, mighty as it is, is finite and can be measured; but grace, which is now beginning to stream forth like a river into which the new believers are to be submerged, is infinite and immeasurable, for it flows from eternal life to eternal life.

1:29. *The next day he saw Jesus coming toward him, and said, "Behold, the Lamb of God, who takes away the sin of the world!"*

He does not say: Behold, the Son, but: *Behold, the Lamb*. Neither does he say: who will take away the sin of the world, but: *who takes away*. And this though Christ is not yet on the Cross, does not yet suffer, has not yet really begun. He does not say: the Son, because he does not want to interfere in his self-revelation or anticipate him. This again is a sign of tactfulness, that he refrains from saying it.

He does not enlarge on his knowledge about the Son of God. He says to him: I know that you are innocent and that your being can be expressed now only by two contrasting words: innocence and sin. Were John to speak of the Son, he would have to expound the relationship between Father and Son. But he has no intention of expounding anything; he simply wants to summarize and draw all attention to the center, which is Christ; he does so by contrasting sin with the taking away of sin. He sees the essence of the Lord in this taking away of sin, and he sees his whole way in this. He is aware that the Lord is not merely one who is innocent, but that he is *the Lamb*. He carries, not one particular sin, but *the sin of the world*; not a partial remission is meant, but a total taking away. He does not mention again to the Lord what he has said before: that he is unworthy, that he baptizes only with water. For the Lord is now here and knows everything. John has no need to introduce himself to him through signs of humility. His relationship to Christ is so clear that no words are needed. And John's integrity is such as to need no excuses. Were he to profess his unworthiness at this moment, this would be doubt and ingratitude. He had to speak in this way in front of the others. Now he only says: You are. In recognizing your greatness, I do not need to emphasize my nothingness.

1:30. *This is he of whom I said, "After me comes a man who ranks before me, for he was before me."*

This sentence repeats verse 15. In the first case, it is a testimony given about Jesus. Now the testimony is restated; it is to remain but enriched with the new meaning of the Lamb of God and the sin of the world.* As taking away the sin of

---

* Christ was the Lamb of God already before he had taken away the sin of the world.

the world, he follows on after the Baptist, but he precedes him as the Lamb of God. Already as Son in the Father, he was the Lamb of God; his whole way existed already in the Father. His mission is not temporal; it is already perfected before its beginning. Certainly there is a moment in history in which he suffers. But it is preceded by the timelessness in the bosom of God. Everything eternal taking place in time is itself beyond time and before all time. The greater and deeper something is, the more timeless it is. The Lord precedes men; the good precedes the mediocre; achievement precedes inactivity. Everything heavenly precedes the earthly. What is timeless is the real; the temporal is only a shadow of it. We borrow from eternity the time in which we work and act. But in doing this, we forget that we have only borrowed it and attribute to it a meaning of its own that it does not have. The true meaning of time is eternity. The non-Christian sees the Christian life as waste of time, and rightly so, because for him the time of the world is essential and lasting. The Christian, however, sees in time only something that is loaned to him by eternity: everything essential rests securely in the womb beyond time. The Lord's time has from all eternity been loaned from the Father's eternity, and apart from his abandonment on the Cross, he always beholds time from the angle of eternity.

1:31. *I myself did not know him; but for this I came baptizing with water, that he might be revealed to Israel.*

I, John, did not know him before this, because I am not timeless as he is but have only now come into the world. But I came baptizing with water that he might be revealed to Israel. My task and mission are included in his and can be understood only within his. John stands within time. He has had a childhood during which he only gradually came to recognize the Lord. His encounter with the Lord in his Mother's womb was a kind of baptism for him. Here he received the mission of being the Baptist but not yet the personal awareness of the mission. This awareness came only later. The first was a predestination to which the course of the years added personal recognition. John's mission, of course, had also been eternally decreed in God, and the revelation of the mission took place in the womb at the meeting with Mary, but only later did it become a mission consciously accepted. But for Christ, the mission was from all eternity revealed and accomplished in the bosom of the Father and consciously accepted as such.

1:32–33. *And John bore witness, "I saw the Spirit descend as a dove from heaven and remain on him. I myself did not know him; but he who sent me to baptize with water said to me, 'He on whom you see the Spirit descend and remain, this is he who baptizes with the Holy Spirit.'"*

For John it is perfectly clear from whence the Spirit comes and where he goes. The Trinity is a primary concept for him. He knows the Father. And he saw the Spirit descending in the form of a dove, the symbol of purity, on the Son, who possesses the same purity and now receives that of the Spirit in addition. John knows and understands that each of the three Divine Persons has always had the same qualities as the other two, in equal perfection, but only through their unity are they the perfect Godhead. Each of the three Persons in his uniqueness is perfect, but only in their union are they complete (without any lack being visible in one of them because he is not the two others). This movement of the three to unity is outside of time and indivisible; but from all eternity, this unity becomes three, each having the qualities they all have together. John is also aware that, in spite of their indivisibility, they at times become differentiated. Though one can never describe the Son without saying that he is the Son of God and possesses the Holy Spirit; or the Father without saying that he has the Son in himself and sends out the Spirit; the Spirit cannot be defined in human words at all, because he always is something more than can be perceived: he is the unity, the life, the one poured out going to the one who is sent. He is the possessor and giver of the gifts, but so strongly does he come from the Father and go to the Son and distribute himself to all who desire him that we cannot do justice to him with one single concept. The form of the dove in its inconspicuousness and lack of proportion resembles in some way that of the lamb: both contain in this very inconspicuousness the most sublime qualities. In the Son, this inconspicuousness is related to his mission on earth; in the Spirit, it is related to his indescribable divine essence. Though the three Persons cannot therefore be described without each other, they do at times become distinct, and this happens at the time of the Incarnation of the Son. It is the first time that this happens, and it allows us to perceive their eternal distinction in God. In himself, the Spirit can never be grasped except during the time of the Son's sojourn on earth. The Spirit, of course, remains in the Church after the Resurrection of the Son. But he becomes visible only during that portion of time when the Son is separate from the Father on earth, when the unity of God opens out and we can see in the cleft the relations between the Persons.

John says: *I myself did not know him; but he who sent me to baptize with water said to me.* He gives no clue who it was that spoke to him and sent him to baptize with water. The one who sends is both Father and Spirit, in the unique oneness they possess while the Son is on earth, during which they can almost be said to form Two in One in heaven. During this time, they are in some way left behind; they are those who remain. Ultimately, all mission always comes from the Father; he sends the Son and the Spirit. But here the one who sends is the Father and Spirit in unity. Nevertheless, the one who sends says that John will see the Spirit descend. He does not say: you will see me or us descend, but objectively: the Holy Spirit. The unity of Father and Spirit speaks of the two Persons as if each were a unity in himself.

Here something becomes visible that is essential to all mission. Everyone sent in the Church, especially the priest, who is sent to announce the Word and to baptize and confer the sacraments, receives this mission from the Father. But he does not really know the Father; he has not seen him. But he knows the Son; he can grasp him; the Son is his Way. So he will rely much more on the Son regarding his mission than on the Father, consult with him about it, and look at it as received from the Son. He receives it in reality from the Father, but the Father makes of it a gift to the Son. It is the Father who seeks helpers for the Son, and the Son is the one who accepts them. The priest is sent to preach and confer the sacraments; both are effects of the Holy Spirit. It is the Spirit who allows the Word to be proclaimed; he it is who allows the sacraments to be effective. Those who are sent distribute in the Eucharist the Body of the Lord, but without the Holy Spirit, this Body would not be effective because it would be lacking in two things: the Spirit in the Son (and in the Host) and the Spirit in the conferring of the sacrament.

In the same way, any mission in the Church proceeds from the Father to the Son through the Holy Spirit. When John sees the Spirit descend on the Lord, he sees first of all two within the Trinity, then the mission of the Spirit to the Son, and finally the Spirit remaining on the Son. He sees something more in the Son than he would have seen otherwise; he sees as the distinguishing mark of the Son the Spirit who unites him with the Father. He sees the unity of Son and Spirit. Twice, therefore, he sees two: the unity of Father and Spirit, then the unity of Son and Spirit, and in between the movement from Father to Son in the Spirit, the transition in God that becomes visible here in the Incarnation.

I myself did not know him. He means the Son. John does not know the Son because he does not yet know on whom the Spirit will descend. He only knows: the one who was part of the one who spoke in my ear will become visible to my eye in the form of a dove. From this he can conclude that he will see what he has heard. And he sees in the visible signs the Spirit in his movement to the Son and the Spirit remaining in the Son; by the power of this Spirit, the Son now baptizes, not in water only, but also in the Spirit. The Son himself is the first sacrament, and he inaugurates the sacraments. John baptized with water only; that was his mission. But he was sent at the same time by the Spirit to behold with his eyes the inauguration of the baptism in the Spirit: he sees with his own eyes the process in which this sacrament is instituted. Those coming later will no longer see the Spirit in the sacrament but will receive him in faith only. They have no need of seeing him, for from now on there exists baptism in the Spirit. The Spirit no longer descends; he is here and remains on the Lord. Until now, water was merely a symbol of the purifying power; from now on, it becomes the sign of the Spirit. In this institution of the first sacrament, a vision is contained, the vision of John. It will from now on not take place in a differentiated vision but within faith, as part of faith. In the institution of the other sacraments, for example, the Eucharist or penance, no such vision of the Spirit will take place; they are proclaimed by the Lord alone and instituted in faith in the Lord.

1:34. *And I have seen and have borne witness that this is the Son of God.*

Once more the vision is stressed. Through this vision and at the very moment it takes place, there begins together with the institution of the sacrament also the true witness to and proclamation of the Word of God; this one is the Son of God, the promised One, announced by Father and Spirit. Here, too, there is the unity of recognition in vision and hearing in faith. John testifies that the Father and Spirit have told him this and that he has believed their voice but also that he found his believing confirmed in the vision of the Spirit; the equation between hearing and seeing could be made. What he confirms is that Christ is the *Son of God*, and this because he has the Holy Spirit as something belonging to himself so that he can mediate him to the world. Only because Christ mediates the Spirit, whom he possesses as his very own, can others afterward also mediate this Spirit, whom they do not possess as their own possession.

The remaining of the dove signifies that the Spirit remains after being mediated and distributed in the sacrament; he here resembles the Eucharist, which in spite of being distributed always remains whole and entire. He resembles the Eucharist also in the fact that the Spirit acts sovereignly in this distribution and does not depend on the one receiving him. The effect is not proportionate to the disposition of the recipient. Even in confession, where a subjective openness is required, not only the absolution but already the confession transcends the subjective. In confessing, an opening takes place that belongs already to the sacramental grace going beyond what the sinner has subjectively been willing to achieve.

THE CALL OF THE DISCIPLES

1:35–36. *The next day again John was standing with two of his disciples; and he looked at Jesus as he walked, and said, "Behold, the Lamb of God!"*

We are told that John has disciples. Disciples of his own, his disciples. There are men in the Church who have disciples and who bring these disciples to the Lord. There is this Catholic possibility of having disciples; every priest and every layman can have it. John keeps these disciples until the call comes, and the call makes itself heard at the moment when the Lord appears. John together with his disciples sees the Lord passing by. For the disciples, it is the first encounter with Jesus. John points him out and says: *Behold, the Lamb of God*. Yesterday when he alone met the Lord, he had added: *who takes away the sin of the world*. Today he omits these words. He wants the disciples to go to the Lord uninhibited by calculations about their personal perfection or sin. Speculation about the taking away of sin would include the perspective of their own part in it; the whole of salvation history would present itself, the necessity of cooperation. But the disciples are not meant to come to the Lord with these perspectives. They are to become converted in naked faith and pure love. They are not to think about personal security and salvation. No calculating attitude must arise. They must be totally surrendered. Those who show them the way must help them to accomplish this surrender, must accompany them until the moment comes when they dare to take the plunge and lose themselves in order to offer themselves completely.

1:37. *The two disciples heard him say this, and they followed Jesus.*
For the first time, men leave a merely human commitment in order to enter a Christian one. It is a conversion. Until now they were bound to a human master, and this commitment was good and pleasing to God. But they leave it behind in order to enter a greater one. This transition is a plunge, not a gradual development. It is not like passing from one teacher to another, from the teacher of the junior grade to that of the seniors. It is the choice of the absolute made in total love. Their first teacher was a good teacher, for he enabled them to make this choice. And they themselves know that by placing themselves at the Lord's disposal they fulfill at the same time the will of their first teacher. There is, then, a human education toward the Lord, and this must be so. It is permitted to men to bind people to themselves for the sake of the Lord. Those missionaries who made themselves like foreign peoples in human ways in order to win influence over them and by this means lead them to the Lord were right in doing so. They formed human bonds in order to transform them into divine ones. When the Church sometimes mistrusted their methods and even recalled them, this obedience with which they sacrificed their work surely was something glorious, but, in recalling them, the Church was lacking in obedience and in knowledge of the ways of the Lord.

John, who trains his disciples and then hands them over to the Lord, remains wholly within the Lord's mission. In binding them to himself and in letting them go, he fulfills the Lord's will. His disciples do not know before their conversion that they have a task from the Lord, but they are already included in it. They are marked out before they are aware of it. For the present, they would not be able to understand or endure it. They still live within a finite horizon, but the mark they have received contains the possibility of a growth beyond all horizons. A vocation to the Church, to an order, to the priesthood, or to any other special mission is already at work in the soul long before the soul becomes conscious of it. It is not given at the moment of conversion; the conversion is merely the soul's becoming conscious of what God has planned for it from eternity. The disciples followed Jesus. In this first following, no test, selection, or assignment of tasks takes place. They simply follow, and because they do so, they are accepted. This following precedes every election.

The apostle John is among those who follow; he is the one who is called first because he represents love. There is no vocation, no choice or office, except on the foundation of love, which is already laid. Thus it is always in the Catholic Church. The disciples follow the Lord, and it is not stated where, how far, how long. It is a simple bond, forever. Had they not received the Baptist's indication, they would have had every excuse for themselves: they were not sent; only their attention was drawn. No obligation was laid on them. They did not know the Lord. But John thinks them mature enough to know what they must do. From the moment in which they really begin to move and follow the Lord, it would be sin not to go farther, not to go to the end. This is true for all converts who are on their way to the Lord. Once the first step has been taken and one has begun to move forward, one cannot go back. All other steps have to follow. This applies also to all other vocations the Lord gives within the Church.

1:38–39. *Jesus turned, and saw them following, and said to them, "What do you seek?" And they said to him, "Rabbi" (which means Teacher), "where are you staying?" He said to them, "Come and see." They came and saw where he was staying; and they stayed with him that day, for it was about the tenth hour.*

The disciples follow behind the Lord and do not make themselves known. They do not call out to him; they do not try to catch up with him. They know the humility of a pure and simple following. Nor do they ask themselves what is going to happen now. The decision rests wholly with the Lord. The Lord himself turns around and addresses them. He allows them to come to him; he is ready for them. To everyone who follows he gives at once the whole. No one can say that he has followed the Lord without the Lord having turned around and taken notice of him. And it never happens that the Lord allows a man to run until he has caught up with him and reached him. Rather, every life that follows him is fulfilled and led by him. Not in the sense of sensible consolation; it can be a fulfillment in the night and in aridity. The how of fulfillment is a matter for the Lord. The manner of its taking place is as unparalleled as the fulfillment is certain. It is further said that the Lord sees them coming. They are walking up to him under his eyes. This gaze of the Lord falls on every moment of our life in which we try to follow him.

"*What do you seek?*" In asking this, he knows that they have found. "*Where are you staying?*" The disciples also know that in their asking they have already found. For by his question, Jesus makes clear to them that they have reached the goal. If they were to answer the question, they would have to answer with their whole lives. In words it is impossible. So they respond with a new question. We are no longer seeking anything; we have already found what we were seeking; but where is your place? The disciples make no condition: they do not ask what his intentions are or where he is going to lead them. They only ask for him whom they have found. *"Come and see."* He acknowledges the bond and seals it. Nothing more can be said about this invitation, because he is perfection. They come with him and see and stay. The whole episode issues in pure light, in a fullness and revelation untranslatable into words. This takes place already in the first meeting with the Lord. With him there is no gradual education; rather, they are immediately overwhelmed by his infinity in a coming and seeing that will never end.

1:40–42. *One of the two who heard John speak, and followed him, was Andrew, Simon Peter's brother. He first found his brother Simon, and said to him, "We have found the Messiah" (which means Christ). He brought him to Jesus. Jesus looked at him, and said, "So you are Simon the son of John? You shall be called Cephas" (which means Peter).*

Andrew meets Peter and announces: *"We have found."* This happened as the result of John's word. Already the first one he meets must share. Every grace from the Lord must be passed on at once. It is the first apostolate that the disciples exercise. No arguments are delivered, only the testimony: *We have found.* A sentence is sufficient; in this first situation, everything is quite simple and transparent. The words still have their full weight, their full impact; they are therefore used sparingly; things can be called by their name. The scene has the primitive quality of untarnished conviction. It leads directly to the meeting with Jesus and the change of name for Peter. This is the first effect of the following of Christ: it is the Lord who from now on bestows the name on the disciple he accepts. He becomes a different man. The acceptance takes place with elementary force. Any superfluity or ceremony is left aside;

everything has a totally new and hitherto unexperienced power and efficacy. There are no calculations, comparisons, or securities. It was like this in the first immediate meeting between God and man. Today, by contrast, so many words are needed that are powerless for the sole reason that we no longer want to expose ourselves to the naked impact of the Lord. We cannot endure this immediacy. The first disciples, even though later on they will fall into sin again, live in the immediacy of faith. Our distance from the Lord is caused by ourselves alone, for the presence of the Lord and its immediate impact have not diminished.

In the following of the two first disciples, everything was love: without a word, they were admitted into the Lord's intimacy. In the meeting with Peter, there occurs an institution, a choice; a destiny is decided. It is a question of office. The two first disciples simply follow; the whole is a movement of surrender and being accepted. Peter, however, comes before the Lord and is in this meeting appointed to his new office. He does not come of his own account, as the disciple of love did; he is brought along. But he comes as the one who is destined to embody the element of the institutional in the community, which is still without form. As soon as he comes on the scene, as soon as the Lord gives him his name, the structure of the future Church is raised in the person of this unknown man. The official element in Peter does not grow or develop. It is present, created by the will of the Lord, personified in this man whom he has marked out, who bears the seal of office. The bystanders need not be aware of it; for them, there is simply one more who joins the group. That he already has now a certain power over them they know as little as he himself knows it. But it exists nonetheless, hidden from both parts. There are lots of people already under the power of the pope unknown to themselves and to him, especially the baptized Christians outside the Church and, in a wider sense, also all the unbaptized who are called to baptism by the Lord. The office is merely indicated and cannot yet be described. It is still totally undifferentiated. But it is already the same office as today, where it has become subdivided into a multitude of individual functions and appears differentiated. Already at the moment when Peter becomes the Rock, he is burdened with the Church. The Church is the total burden of every Christian, but this burden finds its official expression in the Rock. The Church is the burden of everyone, for no one is dispensable in the Church, and no one is authorized to pass the burden on to other Christians. Each one has his personal mission in the Church; this is the office entrusted to him by the Lord. When the Lord assigns the burden of the ecclesial office to Peter, his whole person is claimed for this office. Christians honor in Peter and in every priest the office, not the person, but everyone holding a hierarchical office in the Church must know that he himself may not separate the office from the person. For the Lord's mission is unique and indivisible and always a mission of love. The Lord himself was sent by the Father solely in love, and his office was one of love. There must be no separation or tension in the Church between office and love.

Peter is the Rock. He is the foundation and the summing up of all that is official in the Church. He is that firm ground on which the building can be raised. His task is to give to the boundlessness of love a structure that is visible in the world. If love alone were to rule supreme without the office, everything would dissolve, everyone would proceed according to his own inspiration and judgment and would inevitably grow away from the unity of the Church. Love needs a norm for its orientation, and this norm must be firm and at times severe. This side also belongs to love. Without the Rock of Peter, love in the Church would become vague and formless. In the Rock it finds its unity; in its order the personal outlook becomes enlarged, and unfettered individual love fits itself into the order of love as service in the community. Everything receives a firm objective structure within which the life of love can develop as a healthy life. From now on, there exist Christian names: Cephas, Rock, the disciple will be called. As the Lord was already called the foundation stone, which is broken and crumbles into numberless fragments in order to become the whole and the fullness, so also the Rock of Peter, the head of the hierarchy, will be shared out in numberless fragments, but everything returns to the head and thus to unity.

1:43. *The next day Jesus decided to go to Galilee. And he found Philip and said to him, "Follow me."*

The two first disciples followed the Lord of their own accord. The third is led to him; the fourth he meets by chance. The formalities become shorter because the Lord is already surrounded by apostles; there is already a movement to which only additions have to be made. The meeting seems now almost to be left to chance. The following in itself amounted to so very little measured against the weight of the calling; it is even less to be led to the Lord and still less if one is taken along by chance. Almost nothing is sufficient from our side; grace does everything. Man's goodwill counts for almost nothing. Advertising and organization in the Church almost count for nothing in the face of a simple meeting with the Lord, as if by chance. The following into which Philip is invited is not clearly specified. It is not evident to what one obliges oneself. One single word includes the whole way that lies ahead. It is not a following according to a plan or a mutual agreement. It is absolute and at the same time the most manly thing that exists.

1:44-45. *Now Philip was from Bethsaida, the city of Andrew and Peter. Philip found Nathanael, and said to him, "We have found him of whom Moses in the law and also the prophets wrote, Jesus of Nazareth, the son of Joseph."*

The first recruiting of the disciples was easy, for it took place among blood brothers. Now for the first time an outsider enters the circle. The first confrontation takes place, the first dialogue about the truth of Christianity. Philip does not try to convince in any other way than by witnessing: "*We have found.*" He says, not we have met, but we have found. In this lies for him the strength of the proof. They have found, so they have sought; an openness was in them to accept someone. They were like people knowing that somewhere a task is awaiting them but not knowing of what it consists. At present they can do no more than to be ready for this task, remain in a state that they recognize to be one of seeking without being able to say what it is they are seeking. They know only that they are on a way but that the goal toward which they are walking does not depend on them. They have to be ready for one whom they do not know, about whom they know only that they must be at his disposal. They even have no idea whether they will suit him or not, whether he will seek them or not. All they know is that the whole decision rests with him and in no way with themselves; their only task is to seek him and place themselves at the disposal of him, the unknown. In addition, they know that their openness is the response to a demand already made, that it is the entire and sufficient response. It is this response that matters, and in this point they must not fail. If they fulfill this one thing, openness in order to be able to find, or rather allow themselves to be found, then they have fully done their task. A final point has been put behind their past life. What will happen after this finding and being found will be of a different nature. In this new life, they will forever lag behind their task, for everything will now become infinite and beyond their capacity to understand; every calculation and comprehension will cease. But first there is this finishing point, which will also be a starting point. At this point, demand and fulfillment are one. It is the turning point when the law is fulfilled and the Old Covenant passes over into the New Covenant; a visible and firmly marked point before the eternal movement in the new life of love begins. For one moment there is perfection: what is meant to be exists. Then everything begins to move again, and love will become so quick and will grow to such a degree that man will never be able to come equal with it. The task that the Lord is going to set will always be one that could have been fulfilled more perfectly, because love has no limits in the vertical direction. Now, however, they have found. In this indivisible meeting point between Old and New Covenant, between law and love, they have found the Lord as the one whom they expected together with the law and the prophets: *Jesus of Nazareth, the son of Joseph*. In this encounter they have found their Master, the one who will always remain their Master because to have found him means to go on finding him ever anew and to be allowed to seek him ever anew for all eternity.

1:46. *Nathanael said to him, "Can anything good come out of Nazareth?" Philip said to him, "Come and see."*

Nathanael clothes his doubts in an objective and concrete form. *"Can anything good come out of Nazareth?"* is not a disdainful rejection but an objective evocation of the

THE CALL OF THE DISCIPLES

Tradition, which is expecting the Messiah, not out of Galilee, but from Judea. Philip's answer is equally pragmatic and objective: *"Come and see."* This means follow before you have seen. The vision will come; it will even be the starting point for the whole way to come and already contain it. But in order to reach the vision, the way of blind following must first be entered. It is Philip, who already is an apostle, who says this; the apostle leads people to the Lord by facing them with the objective reality, not by making promises of his own. It is not a question of a certain definite vision or a definite way. The vision has no degrees or limits; it leaves everything open. It must be so wherever someone is called to conversion, to religious life, or in any other way to God. Philip gives no proofs to Nathanael that something good can come out of Nazareth or that Jesus is the Messiah. He only invites him to enter and through this action come to the contemplation that enlightens from within.

Nathanael's question proves that he has not yet reached contemplation. His expectations are for the time being directed to something definite. But promise and fulfillment seldom fall together in the way man expects it. In the human understanding of the divine promise, the pure light of God is most often divided as by a prism: each one takes in what seems in conformity with himself. He chooses a part of the truth because he is unwilling to place himself at the disposal of the whole truth. Nathanael is not prepared to accept that the Messiah could come from Nazareth and Bethlehem at the same time. Instead of being a pure instrument, man interposes his own personality and subjectivity in the reception of the Word. It seems important to him to be involved in it with his own thoughts and considerations. But it is not these that are important; rather, it is the faith that leaves all room to the promise to fulfill itself.

The living faith is what is decisive, and the coloring that of necessity it takes on when it is received by man must remain a side issue. As in heaven, there is more joy over one sinner who becomes converted than over ninety-nine just, so there is more joy in heaven over one believer who makes room for God's freedom to fulfill himself as he wills than over all religious traditions, which try to calculate and establish the possibilities of this fulfillment beforehand. From the premises known to us, we can never deduce anything that could limit or determine God's action in any direction—even when the fulfillment God accords to his promises is always the best and right one. Man's openness to any fulfillment that comes from God is contemplative faith in which God shows at any moment as much as is necessary of himself in order for faith to become a living and vibrant one.

1:47–48. *Jesus saw Nathanael coming to him, and said of him, "Behold, an Israelite indeed, in whom is no guile!" Nathanael said to him, "How do you know me?" Jesus answered him, "Before Philip called you, when you were under the fig tree, I saw you."*

Jesus recognizes the approaching disciple and knows there is nothing false in him. It is characteristic of his judgment to rest on his insight into the soul. The nearer someone is to the Lord, the more capable he is of looking through others. There are, of course, people who from a naïve ignorance of evil do not see and recognize the lie in someone else. There are the naïve Christians who in good faith see only good in others. These are not fit for action; they should live their lives in contemplation. Only a knowledge that in love also sees what is evil gives a right to action, but without giving at the same time the right to renounce contemplation. Jesus, who sees and sees through

Nathanael, is in action. His action, however, always proceeds from contemplation. There is a superabundance of contemplation in his life: eternity before his birth, the thirty hidden years, the desert, the nights of prayer during his active life and before his Passion. Every strength to suffer, every power of surrender he draws from the Father. Contemplation is a beholding and reflecting of truths that lie not in us but in God. In contemplation, God gives the sinner something that lifts him above the sin and carries him to a higher level than the one natural to him. The divine element is strengthened in man, but not only this, God also gives him something better on the human level. He gives him many things that he needs for his earthly pilgrimage in his mission but that he does not possess by nature. The Lord himself meditates as a man; he, too, needs the lifeline to the Father that every man should have. So he also receives in contemplation gifts from the Father that are meant for him as a man, gifts that he possesses as Son of God but that he has to receive in a new way from the Father as Son of Man. Among these gifts is the possibility of passing from the contemplative vision of people to true action for and in them.

The Lord's encounter with Nathanael is the encounter of the Lord's vision with that of Nathanael. In the encounter, Nathanael stands at the beginning of contemplative vision. Philip has promised it to him, and the Lord is presently going to renew the promise. But first the disciple has to enter into the Lord's vision and be assessed in it. Already before entering into the act of passing judgment, Jesus has seen and assessed the disciple in his vision. The judgment he now makes is the fruit of the vision he had of him as he was under the fig tree. In this being seen by the Lord, Nathanael himself sees the Lord. Through his vision of the Lord, he comes to faith. On this process of infinite significance rests all the power of prayer in the Church and the entire justification of the Church's contemplative orders. All coming to the Lord and to faith, all active leading to the Lord, is contained in and made possible by this original contemplation. Nathanael is the first who finds his faith through the Lord's contemplation. The fulfillment is given before the expectation is felt. Through his mention of the fig tree in this first instant, the Lord gives proof that it is vision that can lead to faith. Nathanael receives the visible proof; those who follow after can always refer to this first proof.

1:49. *Nathanael answered him, "Rabbi, you are the Son of God! You are the King of Israel!"*

The proof that the Lord gives is an answer to Nathanael's longing for something that was unattainable until it found faith. But at the moment of Nathanael's coming to faith and the fulfillment of his longing, he becomes aware that this longing grows to even more infinite proportions. In every contemplation, this double movement occurs: the longing for God is fulfilled and at the same time enlarged to more consuming longing. Any word of the Lord is sufficient to kindle in us this fire. And this fire is the form in which human contemplation hands itself over to the Lord's contemplation; the small vision pours itself out into the ocean of God's infinite vision. This surrender has almost something romantic about it. Young persons in their years of development are capable of opening themselves enthusiastically and entirely to an ideal. They are able to do this because their life has not yet received a definite form or clearly defined program. They wax enthusiastic for anything great and surpassing that they meet. But it is the Lord who shows what is most surpassing, and in the vision of this greatest a man can remain young forever. He can give himself, throw himself into it with all his soul. A young person in his enthusiasm wants to conquer life and enjoy it, but the longing for God wants to be at the disposal and service of his eternal destiny. This makes the difference; the force of surrender is the same.

1:50–51. *Jesus answered him, "Because I said to you, I saw you under the fig tree, do you believe? You shall see greater things than these." And he said to him, "Truly, truly, I say to you, you will see heaven opened, and the angels of God ascending and descending upon the Son of man."*

The Lord affirms that his own vision is all-embracing and that in the disciple's surrender of the limited vision into the greater infinite vision, faith is found and with it truth. Nathanael believes because the Lord said to him that he had been seen by the Lord. Having surrendered his limited vision to the vision of the Lord without seeing it himself, merely in response to the Lord's affirmation of his vision: that is his faith. But this faith will open new vistas to him. He will see the Ever Greater that is the Lord. Because he believes, he has opened himself for what is greater, for faith and openness are the same. But he was open for faith because nothing in him contradicted love— that is the absence of falsehood in him. He was prepared in love to open himself in faith. Every impurity in the soul is a hindrance to faith, but faith and love form an inseparable unity. If a man were to train himself to highest ethical purity but without love, then this purity would never obtain faith for him. But if he were to love intensely though without being free from sin, this love would prepare in him a deeper level of order that would make the disorder of sin appear more easily removable. Love is the most important of all; without love, there can be no faith. Because the disciple believes in love, he will see greater things. Through love he is open to faith and so prepared for any further road, and this road leads straight to heaven. *"You will see heaven opened."* For those who believe, heaven stands open, though not for all in the same way. But as believers, all share in the mysteries of heaven. That heaven is opened to them means that from now on they will accept as believers everything coming from heaven. It does not mean that they will understand all the mysteries of heaven. But the door is opened for this. They accept everything heavenly, even though they cannot grasp it all. For they know once and forever: God is greater. There exists a real possibility to go from earth to heaven. No longer is heaven closed and God enthroned at a distance to which no one can have access. There is a coming and going, an ascending and descending. The Lord simply says: *"You will see heaven opened."* He does not add "above you" (or something else); this would create a new distance, would require the effort of looking up, suggest a ladder. But heaven is no longer something high above us; it is open, can be reached, is accessible.

"You will see . . . the angels of God ascending and descending." When heaven is opened, one would first expect a movement of descent. But the Son is as much on earth as he is in heaven, so that both movements are instantaneous and are carried out simultaneously. The angels here can be a symbol for the Holy Spirit, who comes down from the Father to the Son dwelling among us, but also to the Son who as God is in heaven. We see the Son now dwelling among us on earth, but even though he is so much among us, he has never left heaven. If Nathanael had no faith, he would see the Lord in only his human qualities. As a believer, he will see him with the angels. Angels are beings who have no human substance and never can. Only a believer can see angels. This makes clear that a mere

historical faith, a liberal faith in mere facts, has nothing to do with real faith. This real faith is of such a kind that it sees everything through love, the angels also. This vision need not be seen with the eyes, though there will in fact always be some people who see angels with their eyes. Nathanael perhaps never was one of them.

THE MARRIAGE AT CANA

2:1–12. *On the third day there was a marriage at Cana in Galilee, and the mother of Jesus was there; Jesus also was invited to the marriage, with his disciples. When the wine failed, the mother of Jesus said to him, "They have no wine." And Jesus said to her, "O woman, what have you to do with me? My hour has not yet come." His mother said to the servants, "Do whatever he tells you." Now six stone jars were standing there, for the Jewish rites of purification, each holding twenty or thirty gallons. Jesus said to them, "Fill the jars with water." And they filled them up to the brim. He said to them, "Now draw some out, and take it to the steward of the feast." So they took it. When the steward of the feast tasted the water now become wine, and did not know where it came from (though the servants who had drawn the water knew), the steward of the feast called the bridegroom and said to him, "Every man serves the good wine first; and when men have drunk freely, then the poor wine; but you have kept the good wine until now." This, the first of his signs, Jesus did at Cana in Galilee, and manifested his glory; and his disciples believed in him. After this he went down to Capernaum, with his mother and his brethren and his disciples; and there they stayed for a few days.*

The Lord does not overwhelm his own at once with the greater things, with the vision he has promised. Nothing is precipitated. They are left for three days in faith, waiting for vision. These are the days of contemplation without seeing. For the disciples, vision comes on the third day; as far as we are concerned, we may have to remain waiting indefinitely. If for the disciples to whom vision was promised there is nothing to see for the present—and three days is a long spell in the short time the Lord remains on earth—we should control our impatience and curiosity. The third day has a link with Easter. On this day, the beginning is made; here the beginning of vision, at Easter the beginning of resurrection. At Easter, too, three days pass between faith and vision, and in between there lies the suspended phase of waiting. In spite of this waiting, the third day means the totally unexpected. The kind and manner of the communication are always unpredictable. There is the same disproportion between expectation and fulfillment as there is between man's question and God's response. This response often appears as a disappointment, but only because it has not been understood. Once it is understood, however, it is found to contain more than one had ever expected; it surpasses the greatest that could have been expected. The disciples were thinking perhaps that they were expecting a big, sensational deed; perhaps they expected to see angels, something in line with the great words of the promise. Instead of this, the absolute miracle occurs, a stark miracle not clothed in human terms. Perhaps it would have been all the same to them at this moment to have had water to drink instead of wine. Now they are offered this wine, the result of a pure miracle, which is always possible without any preparation and out of any proportion. At Easter they will perhaps expect their own resurrection and receive instead something seemingly less important, something prosaic and very simple: the sacrament of confession. But this very ordinary thing is the greatest. We can hardly imagine the splendor of the resurrection that the disciples expected. But they have to die like everyone else. Yet they are redeemed from every sin through the gift of confession. That it is sufficient to go to confession, to perform this inconspicuous action in faith in the Lord, that is the greatest. And when the Lord at this moment gives the command to fill the jars, this seemingly inconspicuous action also becomes a sublime revelation of his glory. For he fills the jars with water as much as he fills the emptiness that waits for him with grace.

He is redeemed who in faith performs his action and simply does what is expected of him. These here drink the water changed into wine; those others confess their sins and receive absolution. Both miracles take place on behalf of those who are present with faith in their hearts. Nothing more is expected of men than obedience in the small, inconspicuous actions that the Lord needs for the revelation of his glory and for which he asks.

He does not work the miracle without the mediation of men. In both cases, he needs servants: here to fill the jars, in the other case to hear confessions. For he usually mediates his gifts through men. Already the grace of his coming he mediated through his Mother and chose in her, the All-Pure, the Mediatrix par excellence: for the time of his coming, his staying on earth, and for eternity.

It is not by chance that water is turned into wine, for later the wine will be turned into blood. In every one of the Lord's miracles, a link with the sacraments becomes visible. All miracles are connected among themselves, each with those that went before and those that come after, and also with the whole visible life of the Lord. All miracles complement each other in the same way as also the sacraments complement and include each other. The miracles are predictions of the sacraments as they also are foreshadowings of his own life journey, and each is a completion of his task. Every miracle contains in some way everything he gives us; it is not just one single ray from his sun but a whole bundle of rays, and each of them leads back to his unique and total self in each of his individual actions. Thus, the miracles take place for his glorification insofar as they powerfully force us to see where and who he is. They are instructions that are meant to be understood, not individually, but rather in their interconnection; this connection is the Lord himself. In their totality, they give a perfect picture of the Lord and in particular of him as the Lord of the sacraments. In the miracles, the sacramentality of our Lord's earthly existence can be read. The miracles are part of the strengthening of faith in the sacraments and so belong in a special way to the sacrament of confirmation. We are always looking for proofs of our faith; we are far removed from those who followed in pure faith and believed while simply following. The Lord acknowledges our weakness and leaves us in his miracles such a superabundance of proofs that even the grumblers are compelled to give in and believe. He leaves us this proof permanently: even the grumblers of today would have before their eyes enough proofs revealing the glory of the Lord and compelling their faith, quite apart from the miracles told in the Gospel.

The mother of Jesus was there. It is the first mention of the Mother of God in John. It is characteristic for John that he begins to speak of Mother and Son in a situation that is one of love. Mother and Son are together, and the Mother knows that the Son's hour has come. She knows: it is the beginning of the mission that is to be revealed. She also knows that it is part of her personal mission to point out and fix the hour. Long before this, she was part of the hour of his conception: through her immediate consent, she took part in the decision about this hour. The hour of his birth was also dependent on her, for as his Mother, she caused her child to be born. Now the hour of his mission has come; here, too, she will have to utter her word. In her word of consent to the Spirit, she began to determine the Lord's hour; what was of the Spirit became a body in her. The hour of birth determined the bodily aspect, and through the sphere of the body she returns to the Spirit, who remains her constant companion whom she never leaves, because she always lives in God: the Father has chosen and destined her, the Son passed through her, but the Spirit remains resting on her. Thus, she becomes in the Spirit the companion of her Son, who does everything he does in the Spirit and through the Spirit. The hour that has come is the hour when the Son's mission is to be revealed. The Spirit has fixed this hour, and the Mother also participates in this decision. But she sees the hour in a way she can and must see it as woman and as Mother. She sees it of necessity in a different light from her Son. All that went before was in her eyes grace in the state of waiting; now the mission begins to unroll: the final act can no longer be halted. The opening scene is an unexpected one: it is a feast. For the Mother, there exists an absolute tension between the feast, in which she exteriorly participates, and the beginning of the Passion. For it is thus she sees the beginning of the mission: every glorification of her Son, every fulfillment of a task by him drives him inexorably into the Passion.

It belongs to her mission as Mother that in the same way that she had to give her consent to his conception, so she now has to give a new consent to his public development, to his mission as man. That it is in the midst of a feast that the Mother has to give this consent becomes a symbol for all Christian feasts, which are never complete and finished in themselves. They seem to celebrate only something definite here and now, but they are always the cause of something that lies in the future. The real distinction of a Christian feast in comparison with any other feast lies in the fact that as feast it is to be fruitful forever.

It is to be enjoyed as fruit, but it has to work as seed. Even though its content is something definite and limited, the meaning of a Christian feast is something that is growing, that is infinite.

The Mother bore the Son in her womb and allowed him to grow. In the same way, her indication now symbolizes the maternal shell that remains even when the Son grows away from her and his destiny develops separately from hers. That it is for her the beginning of the painful phase is underlined by the Son in his question: "*O woman, what have you to do with me?*" He makes it clear to her that he is coming forth now solely as God's Son in his mission from the Father. She lets go of him by saying that they have no more wine—for through this word she herself becomes the immediate cause that sets his mission in motion—she, so to say, gives him birth into his mission. He confirms this parting by his separating word. He adds, "*My hour has not yet come.*" With the first word, he draws the closing line behind the past; but the second word, which seems to contradict it, does not open the future. The same apparent contradiction is seen in the fact that he seemingly rejects the petition and then immediately fulfills it. He fulfills it because the Mother gives everything totally back to him and leaves it to him. She does not withdraw her suggestion; neither does she insist on it. She leaves it to him to do what he wills and says in this sense to the servants, "*Do whatever he tells you.*" Here she becomes the symbol of woman in general: she shows to man what she sees as woman and what he as man perhaps has not paid attention to, but the man then responds to what has been shown in his own way.

As woman, she always sees at once the ultimate destiny; she looks through everything else to the catastrophe. For her, the Son's sacrifice is already being enacted; she sees the Cross erected. Everything that is exterior revelation of his glory is for her already the Cross. He as man sees it differently. For him, there exists a time for work, separated from the Passion. This time has already begun with the gathering of the disciples. The hour of suffering, which has not yet come for the Son, will unite them again, Mother and Son. Now, however, is the time for manly work. Mary lives always with the Cross at the back of her mind; she is a woman. The Son, because he is a man, lives toward the Cross ahead of him.

Mother and Son meet here at a marriage feast of strangers. Their united presence at this feast is the beginning and inauguration of a mystery that will later become the Christian sacrament of marriage. That is the reason why the Lord and his Mother stand here opposite each other as man and woman. Until now, Mary was the Mother, the elder and the giver. Later, the Son will grow more and more beyond her, and she will become, so to say, his younger bride. Here at the beginning of the public life, they meet each other on a kind of equal level: he is the adult man, the Son who has become independent, and she is by his side as helpmate, counselor, and friend. Because they embody here the roles of man and woman, their behavior is differentiated, male and female. Woman is the one who watches, cares, inspires, and points out; man is the one who acts according to his own mind and in independence. It is the same in marriage: woman stands in the background; through her inspiration, she feeds the spiritual life of her husband; she shows him what he might otherwise not notice, but if her husband has the mind of a Christian, she must leave it at that and not try to make the decision herself. She should make the decision only if the husband does not think as a Christian. Nor must the woman expect that her suggestions should be carried out

THE MARRIAGE AT CANA 47

fully and in every detail by her husband. She should leave a certain scope in making her suggestions within which the man keeps his freedom.

The Lord's reply to his Mother's comment is harsh. It underlines the difference between their points of view. Of course, there is no question of the Mother's wishing to force a miracle against the will of her Son. In spite of their different ways of seeing, their wills are united. For the Mother only makes a suggestion; she totally places her will into that of her Son. She says to the servants, *"Do whatever he tells you."* She is simply carrying out her own mission from God: to see the needs of men with maternal eyes and draw her Son's attention to them; as soon as she has done her part, she leaves everything to the will of her Son. She knows it is enough that she has mentioned it and that his attention has been drawn to it. What he will make of it is wholly his business. A man's reply to a woman's suggestion is not infrequently harsh. This is the result of his character as the male, who plans and decides and is perhaps otherwise engaged. He has first to assimilate the woman's suggestion and see what he can do with it within his own plan. The Lord also knows about the mystery of their separation, which is now beginning; he sees that the Mother's passion is already at hand, and he neither may nor wants to cover up the pain of separation through accommodating words.

And yet without words of love, they show each other the greatest love. For the Son does in love what the Mother asks for in love and fulfills without succumbing to weakness her love and his own at the same time. In this action of their mutual love, which includes their love of men, they bestow a blessing on the marriage at which they are present. They belong to this marriage and show this belonging by both making use of the servants as if they were their own.

The presence of the Mother at the marriage feast is related in yet another way to the sacrament of marriage: in the sacrament of Cana, the sacrament of the following generations is included. The grace of marriage is not exhausted on the wedding day but embraces the whole of life, the children and their upbringing and their marriage, and so also the children's children. The grace that is beginning to flow here is a stream that overflows the banks of the sacrament. This overflowing prepares the sacrament that is to follow: thus, the Holy Communion of today, if the recipient lives the day in grace, is an advance and overflow toward that of tomorrow. The superabundance of the sacrament is not simply absorbed according to the insufficiency of the state of soul of the recipient; it always gives more grace than man is desiring and expecting. In the same way, when we ask God for something definite, whether he grants it or not, he grants in any case always more than we have desired. This fact is here expressed in the parable of the best wine, later in the superabundance of the multiplication of bread, the miraculous draught of fish. In this overflowing of grace, which exceeds the banks of the sacraments, the Mother has a decisive role. Her total and complete consent, supporting and embracing the consent of the marriage partners, unseals the superabundance of grace.

This grace thus begins to stream in the symbolic action of the miraculous change of water into wine. The water is changed in the jars provided for the purification rites of the Jews. The Lord takes over the ancient rite. He makes use of everything. He allows the ordinary everyday things to enter into the miracle and to continue to exist there. He does not conjure the wine down from heaven; he makes use of what is present. It is a transformation, not a creation. It will be the same with his Blood. That is why the miracle presupposes faith, a faith that is not elicited by what is sensational but sees within the ordinary.

The servants bring the full jars to the steward, who recognizes the wine's special quality without knowing where it has come from. The steward comments on the wine, which he finds to his taste and which fills him with astonishment, as a man not yet touched by grace. His objection is that of one who is not yet a believer and lover, one who raises an objection to grace. He is convinced of the objective quality of the gift, but he is not altogether content; he finds fault with the time or order of things or with something other. To be able to recognize Christian grace, one must already know that it comes from the Father and the Son. It must be accepted in its absolute quality, without making it relative to human standards. The water changed into wine, as also the wine that is going to be changed into Blood in the Eucharist, is not comparable to something better or worse. There is only one Blood of the Lord. It possesses all the qualities that belong to the Lord's Blood and cannot be compared with those of other kinds of blood. There is no sequence or intensification; there is only Blood. And no one can come from outside and impose an order and gradation where Christ has acted. There is his order, which is timeless and whole. We may never count up or compare the measure of grace, but can only receive it, remaining in the Lord. One can measure, weigh, and compare within the Church and the community what is exterior and human, what man can contribute to it, but one can never weigh up what comes from the Lord. It cannot be described or divided. The only thing for man to do to show that he accepts the gift from the Lord and knows where it comes from is what the servants did: believe and in this believing glorify the glory of the Lord.

The steward's remark makes clear that human enjoyments are always followed by dissatisfaction. The more we accumulate them, the less sensitive we become to them. If it is something new that is enjoyed, it brings a momentum of surprise, which later subsides. That is why purely worldly enjoyments become dull, those of the flesh and those of the spirit that do not lead to God and are not open to him. Finally, even in the latter man contents himself with anything as long as it gives distraction and does not leave an opening to God. In contrast to this, the divine gifts are experienced as ever more beautiful the more fully one accepts them, but without it being possible to say that those of yesterday were less beautiful than those of today. God makes the recipient increasingly more receptive and gives more in every gift without a graduated difference being discernible. He increases the capacity to receive and the desire to accept, but comparisons remain impossible. The more God takes possession of the soul, the greater the desire for him he enkindles, but this increase looks ever forward, never backward. The difference between yesterday and today cannot be measured. None can say that he will feel a greater desire for God tomorrow than he does today. The increase is wholly God's and cannot be made relative to time. One does not even dare make the attempt. We cannot say that in today's confession we have to confess weightier or lighter things than in the one that went before. As long as the Christian life remains outside a person as something he wants to come near to, he can "judge" the wine, appraise its value, criticize it or praise it in a positive sense. He can notice a progress from one confession to another. But once he stands within, all comparisons cease for him. Perhaps there are certain things that the priest can and must judge by virtue of his office, but these are not seen by the penitent and are not meant to be seen by him. For God, who has this time given us the grace to avoid "greater sins", it is equally strange that we did not then avoid the small ones, even though these sins from the human standpoint look like a percentage of the former ones. This human way of seeing is ever more effectively taken from us. Seeing with God's eyes increasingly takes away from us any possibility of comparing. In the scene of Cana, we finally have before us the first image of a Christian community. The Lord, his Mother, the disciples, the young couple, the servants, and the people are present. The Mother's presence embodies the presence of the family in the community. The Christian family is not placed in opposition to the community or outside of it; it is part of the community. Every growth of the family will take place in the community. Later, certainly, there will come a separation—there will come a time when the Lord will make a clear distinction between secular and Christian discipleship. But here everything is only at the beginning. It is, first of all, the normal fellowship of the ordinary normal family and the ordinary normal community. The one belongs to the other. The young couple is an anonymous one, symbolizing the numerous others for whom the sacrament of marriage was instituted, who are meant by it and have no need to be called by name: they disappear in the sacrament, which transcends them. The disciples are not yet priests, not yet ordained. Yet even in this embryonic community there already exists the beginning of a hierarchy. On one side stands the Lord with his disciples; on the other, the servants, who do what they are told without demur. Through this obedience, they attain to vision and to belief. But this vision and belief also are on a wholly different level from the vision and belief of the disciples, in which the Lord's promise—"*Come and see*" and "*You shall see greater things than these*"—finds its fulfillment. The faith of the servants is a naïve faith; the faith of the disciples, a faith that sees, for they see in the miracle the promised glory of the Lord. But they see it only in a faith that is open for what is to come. They know who he is; they know that he possesses the glory. They have not given any thought to the how of this revelation. Now they also see that the change of water into wine is part of this revelation. But the real revelation does not exist in this for them. The miracle is more a promise for them than a fulfillment; it is a beginning of revelation, an inchoative one. They behold in it an image of what is to come, a symbol for something else. The Lord himself sees in the miracle already the fulfillment: in water changed into wine, he sees wine changed into Blood. The disciples do not see this, but in the sign they do see the beginning of the mission; they know that the hour has come. They see, not the crown, but one pearl in this crown; they see in the miracle an outward sign for an interior effect. They are also touched by the fact that the servants, who know what has happened, believe. And the biggest impression is perhaps made on them by the Mother's expecting it. Thus, the entire gradation within faith becomes visible: the servants see and believe on account of what they have seen. The disciples believe because they have seen a sign. The Mother believes because she cannot be disappointed and her faith is already a knowing and loving one. Thus, the Lord in a single gesture reveals his glory on different levels at the same time, and each one grasps what he can hold. On this differentiation of the understanding of revelation the difference between visible and invisible Church is based, and so also the sacramental life of the Church as way and transition from visible action to invisible effect of grace outlined. Yet in all this the glory is undivided, in the flesh and in the Spirit, in the transformation and the faith it evokes.

THE CLEANSING OF
THE TEMPLE

2:13–15. *The Passover of the Jews was at hand, and Jesus went up to Jerusalem. In the temple he found those who were selling oxen and sheep and pigeons, and the money-changers at their business. And making a whip of cords, he drove them all, with the sheep and oxen, out of the temple; and he poured out the coins of the money-changers and overturned their tables.*

Jesus enters the temple and finds two realities: the goods and the sellers. But he makes no distinction: he drives them out, the wares as well as the sellers. It is an elementary action: not a sermon, a warning, or an exhortation, but a tempest sweeping all before it. He could have thrown out the sellers and spared the goods. He could have thrown out the goods and spared and instructed the sellers. But he wants neither the one nor the other. He cannot endure this connection between ware and worship or between seller and worship. Any relationship or connection or transition from one to the other is a horror to him. He, who is always ready to welcome sinners, to lead seekers onward, to give the whole to the halfhearted, knows in this case no possible way, no compromise. He wants to make a clear distinction. These salesmen are lacking the right attitude to such a degree that not only does he treat them without gentleness, he also passes them over; he drives them out. They are so engrossed with their own material profit that he is unable to meet them on their level. He enters into relation with anyone who comes to him with a question, a petition, or a sorrow. But he wants nothing to do with these self-satisfied mercenaries who think only of their profit. He is hard as a rock, relentless; he whips them. He is in earnest. From the oxen to the pigeons, from the grossest to the finest, everything is rejected. Nothing of all this can he tolerate here. And he who a few days ago has received the Spirit in the form of a dove, who was compared with the Lamb of God, is not even touched by the symbol and similarity. All trade taking place in the temple precincts is a scandal to him. He wants to show once and for all: there are no business deals in the Church. Here faith and love are demanded and no deals to be made with "friendly powers" that provide gifts or credit of any kind. The action is so radical that it should have sufficed for all future time in memory of the Lord to expel any form of profitmaking from the churches, everything that presents a mixture of cult with trade: simony, abuse of indulgences, and similar things. The Lord knows very well that the Church also has to live and is in need of earthly means; this does not stand to question here, not the offering made at Mass. What is insufferable is the presence in church of people who do not believe, who are not part of it and seek, not the divine, but only their own personal profit. The Lord would never have driven one who is really seeking out of the temple. But the mixture of unbelief and profitmaking is intolerable to him.

So he makes a whip from cords and mercilessly beats these people, he who will later bleed under their merciless lashes. Somewhere in between these two flagellations, the discipline of Christians has its place. They should feel in their flesh the whip of the Lord directed against the constant marketing and bartering of this flesh and its insatiable desire for well-being, coziness, and consumerism in the gross as in the delicate things, against its constant worry of not being the gainer in all situations of life, even in religion itself. In order to turn the marketplace of our fleshly attitude of mind into a temple of God, a dwelling of God's Spirit, we ought not to mind really feeling the Lord's castigation in our flesh. Perhaps we would then in some slight way be taken along on his way to the second flagellation. But in our case, everything, even the sharpest physical penance, remains a symbol, at the most an attempt to show our readiness, never an adequate action, never an imitation of the first or second of the Lord's flagellations.

2:16. *And he told those who sold the pigeons, "Take these things away; you shall not make my Father's house a house of trade."*

After showing his inexorableness, he reopens the possibility of a reconciliation. He offers them a hand. He addresses them. Separate your business from the Church; do not allow your profit-making, your everyday work, your profane thoughts, to accompany you into church. Place into the Father's hands what you bring with you. He does not say: Do not pray for your everyday life and for everything that is important to you and that weighs you down. But: Do not take it inside with you. You must know that what you bring here as prayer no longer belongs to you but is the Father's property. The Father has an ear for it all, but only when you have given it to him. Do not bring it with you as something that is yours, but let it become his when you are in church. And again: do not allow your contemplation to be wholly swallowed up by action; keep a sacred space in your life, and do not immerse yourself in your activity to such a degree that everything becomes profane and your temple a market hall where the Father's voice is drowned by all the turmoil.

2:17. *His disciples remembered that it was written, "Zeal for your house will consume me."*

This Scripture text, as the Lord uses it, stands for the consumption of the house of God itself through the consuming activity of men. He says: You are so consumed with bustle that my house is consumed and nothing remains of its divine glory because of all this human bustle. In consuming my house, you consume me, and that is why I in turn will consume myself for this consumed house of my Father. What should be consumed is our ego by believing, serving, and being subject to love. In this zeal for God, it should consume itself like a piece of wood in the flame. It should be centered, not in itself, but in God's mission. That is the case with our Lord; in him the inimitable, perfect balance of contemplation and action is achieved. Each of his actions corresponds to a vision of the Father, and each vision becomes fruitful in a deed of love. He has his center and point of rest in the Father. In order to know who he himself is, he contemplates the Father. In order to live the life he is meant to live, he lives in the Father. Not only the divinity, eternity, and love belong to both of them together; the humanity also, which he assumed, comes from the Father and goes to him. We never succeed in achieving this balance. To do so, we would have to look unceasingly at the Son as he does at the Father. But this we find too difficult and too strenuous. To do this, we would have to possess love, because love alone can bring about this right balance between contemplation and action; love is the link between the two. But we take care not to be consumed by such love. We choose the easy way out. We select in contemplation and action certain truths of the Son that appear manageable to us and seek to imitate them. Certain actions of his exterior life that appeal to us, certain interior virtues that seem accessible. We pick and choose; we make ourselves a harmless image of the Lord, a dream picture that corresponds to our own liking and is in the last resort only a projection of ourselves. This image appears to be quite honorable; nothing false can be detected in it. Only one trait is missing: life in God, self-consuming in God. It contains only what seems realizable to us with great trouble and labor. But it does not contain the mystery that is beyond our understanding, that which is ever greater: love. If ever it presents itself, we turn away from it because we do not want to acknowledge what we cannot grasp or hear its demand. Did God not give us reason in order that we might be reasonable? Is it possible for us to live always in this consuming zeal; do we not need to recuperate, recover from it within ourselves? In small steps, cautiously, we walk around the decisive point; gradually, and in a hardly noticeable way, we replace God's qualities with our own. God ceases to be the burning issue for the believer; his own faith becomes the important thing; he himself appears as the backdrop and finally becomes the center. The Lord, however, is consumed with zeal at all times; whether in prayer or action, he has God before his eyes. Because our zeal has flagged, we indulge in the false security that God is in us in any case. We are baptized, after all, we believe, and so we are God's temple. Consequently, God will also be in our activity, even when we do not constantly have him before our eyes in the contemplation of his will. In this false security, we make ourselves the center. If formerly we received the sacraments for the sake of God, now gradually we do so also for our own sake and, finally, only for our own sake. If formerly we prayed in order to praise God and serve him, gradually we do so also to find our own satisfaction in it and, at last, only to be on the safe side. Unnoticeably, our whole life with God becomes one single insurance against God's zeal lest it consume us. All disquiet has died away in a devotional indifference that sees in religion no more than a mutual business contract between God and man.

The Lord recognizes his identity in God, and we should recognize ours in the Lord. In him we would come to know who we are: sinners who have been graced by God. But we do not want this; we rather recognize ourselves in ourselves, blocking off any horizon that lies beyond. So it comes to pass that gradually we identify with our sin. We do not want to see our sin in God or give it to the Lord, where it would become manifest as sin. We reserve it for ourselves alone and then cover it up even before our own eyes. In the measure in which we refuse to surrender, we also need to justify ourselves before ourselves, explain away our sin, make our "good will" plausible. We have to lie, and we learn to idealize ourselves in this lie. This is our true sin, and it coincides with our lack of faith, love, and hope. Were we to have a glimmer of understanding of how the road leads from faith over hope to love, we would renounce the lie of our self-image in order to entrust everything to the Lord alone and his transforming love.

2:18. *The Jews then said to him, "What sign have you to show us for doing this?"*

The Jews ask the Lord for a sign, a visible justification for his extraordinary and scandalous behavior. They are prepared to make an exception in his case, to use a yardstick different from the usual one. The extraordinary in Christ, which they regard as negative, is not sufficient for them; they want to see it balanced by the extraordinary of a miracle, which they regard as positive. This would create a balance, and everything would be in good order. If the sign is not granted, they reserve their judgment. Therefore, they do not believe; they want to see the

THE CLEANSING OF THE TEMPLE

reason of every action. They are prepared to use a different measure in his case but do not notice that this measure is still their own. They find themselves very generous in their approach and do not see that what has happened in the temple is in itself the sign of greatness. They take it for an announcement, an introduction, not for the thing itself. They see the superhuman, not in what has happened, but instead in the fact that they are prepared to recognize the power and effect of what has happened if it is balanced by the power and effect of a miracle. It is almost an act of atonement they are demanding for the injustice done to them, and they offer the Lord an opportunity for this. They cannot see that their seemingly generous attitude contains and expresses their own pettiness of mind.

2:19. *Jesus answered them, "Destroy this temple, and in three days I will raise it up."*

Now the Lord in his turn suggests a miracle. He accepts their challenge. But now they do not want to hear, because they have no faith. A faith that rests only on the calculation of what is seen is not faith. Faith is never a sum that works out right. Faith can be evoked by the visibility of a miracle, but no one has the right to make his faith dependent on such a sign. Not even the Jews had a right to this before God, even though the new faith was still so new at the time that one can understand that they could not make up their mind to believe without sensible proofs. But they should not have bartered with God. Christians, too, should not use graces received as a claim to new graces. If the grace is invisible and will perhaps ever remain so, we may never insist on its being made visible but must content ourselves with its invisibility. In whatever form grace comes to us, God demands in every case faith. But when the Lord himself suggests a miracle here, the conclusion cannot be drawn that he would perhaps not have worked it, and the Jews would have been able to strengthen their faith. When God makes an offer, we can be sure that he is prepared to grant faith in what he is going to do. But man cannot lay down conditions of his own. The Lord can create faith through a miracle, but he cannot enter a bargain that would force him to do it. It is precisely this bartering that he has driven out of the temple. That is why the Jews who suggest a bargain have understood nothing; they rather doubt his ability to work the miracle he has offered and remain as closed to the offer as they were to his action before. Every deed of the Lord is an offer; to overlook the one is to refuse the other.

2:20. *The Jews then said, "It has taken forty-six years to build this temple, and will you raise it up in three days?"*

Their outraged exclamation is a statement of their unbelief. They asked for a miracle, a sensational one, to balance the Lord's unbelievable demands. Now that it is offered, they reject it. In their heart of hearts, they know what it is all about. They are not far away from the truth. The temple was built in forty-six years, and the temple of the Lord's body will stand on this earth thirty-three years.

The difference in the number shows that they are not far from the truth. But they do not want to see it, and in this consists their sin.

2:21. *But he spoke of the temple of his body.*

The three days of which he speaks are again the three days between his death and Resurrection. A double equation is made: the first between the destruction and reconstruction of the temple—that is the miracle offered—and the faith of the Jews, which is made conditional on the miracle for which they ask. The second is the destruction and reconstruction of the temple of the body of Christ and our redemption, which is our faith. This redemption is grace granted as consequence of the miracle of the Resurrection; the other miracle is grace offered but not accepted. The temple of stone has become a market hall and is no longer recognized as a temple; it could be torn down that God may be served in newly raised splendor. But this temple is only a symbol of the body of the Lord; this also is not recognized, and it is going to be torn down to its foundations in order to be raised in new glory. In between the parable and the truth there stands a third factor: our sin. It is this sin that will nail the Lord's body to the Cross, will kill him and hurl him down to hell. But it is this sin that will be taken away by the Resurrection in order to make room in us for the building up of faith.

2:22. *When therefore he was raised from the dead, his disciples remembered that he had said this; and they believed the Scripture and the word which Jesus had spoken.*

After the Resurrection of the Lord, the disciples remember these words and believe. Did they not believe before this? Yes, but men do not believe once and for all. We need remembrance, encouragement, stimulation from outside. Remembrance is recollection and enablement of constant construction. The disciples are actively occupied in being disciples, but they need to understand this discipleship in an ever-new way through contemplation. What they have to meditate on is what they have already: their faith. By remembering, they increase their faith. This is another proof that the active life bears in itself the danger of distancing oneself if no time is left for remembrance, remembrance not as nostalgic reminiscence but as a living stone fitted into the building and originating new life. By remembering, the disciples return to the proofs of their faith, proofs that are personal to them: their own life in faith becomes transparent to them; their faith is enlivened. This return is like the souvenir of a sacrament received: they remember the Lord's word like a Communion full of grace. In times of aridity, it is the remembrance of grace received at the time of consolation and becomes the linking together in the Lord of objective remembrance with subjective gratitude even at the time when nothing is felt. Finally, it becomes clear here that in order to come alive, faith must always return to the Lord himself. Otherwise, it becomes mere piety, stifled in itself, in its own exercises, becomes exaggerated sentimentality or the bored accomplishment of Christian "duties".

2:23. *Now when he was in Jerusalem at the Passover feast, many believed in his name when they saw the signs which he did.*

The signs he did are not described to us. We learn only in a negative way why he does them: not in order to lead them to faith, for their kind of faith means nothing to him.

The miracle at Cana was a confirmation of the new faith. Now the new faith is rejected because of the miracle. He does not accept their faith because they want to see miracles according to their thinking. They barter: they offer him their faith for a miracle. They seek sensation; they love rumor and gossip about a miracle. They are quite aware that he can do more than they can. They are perplexed. But they go about it like a mental quiz and assign roles. The faith of the Jews does not resemble the faith of Christians, which has fallen asleep and has grown cold; it is rather an excited, falsely hushed up faith, resting solely on sensation and devoid of hope and love. Its mark is the inclination to play an intellectual game. A sentence is given, and they watch what comes out of it. A countersentence is given at the same time, and again they watch the result.

"The man has powers, so he can work miracles." "The man has no powers, so where do his miracles come from?" There is a simultaneous induction and deduction, both as hypotheses. "In case I should believe, how would his miracles affect me?" Faith and miracle become the material of every kind of philosophical game. The Jews address everything with their intellect alone. The combination of faith and love would appear subjective to them and therefore unrealistic.

2:24–25. *But Jesus did not trust himself to them, because he knew all men and needed no one to bear witness of man; for he himself knew what was in man.*

The Lord wants nothing to do with their game. In the beginning was the Word and not the sign. They believe they can look through the Lord in their intellectual game. But we can look through a man only in love. The Lord knows their innermost heart, but they themselves know nothing. And because he looks through them in their imagined relationship to him, he cannot trust himself to them. If they had no relationship to him, they would not make him the object of their problems; then he would be able to relate to them and give them faith. Faith always comes first from God. Because he loves us first, he lays the foundation of faith in us. We can gain insight into this faith only when we already believe and love. Until then, whatever we may grasp is anything but faith. Faith and love are united and pass into each other. No one can say he believes if he does not love. And if he loves, he also believes, even though he cannot grasp what he believes, even if he thinks his faith is not yet Christian faith. Faith never comes into being without love and cannot exist without love; at most it could be a dead relic in sin. In contrast to this, love can be the beginning of something even without faith, for love always contains the seed of insight, even though one may not yet know what the seed contains. And just as love, so hope also can be a way to faith, though it will find its completeness as true hope only in faith. Both, however, love as much as hope, insofar as they are a prelude to faith, are pure grace with regard to God's offer as also its acceptance by man. A knowledge, however, making faith its object without possessing love and hope remains a deception, a game, even a flight from oneself by the very fact of making oneself and one's own intellectual brilliance the center of attention. Such an addiction to oneself is in reality a flight from oneself. If we concentrate on ourselves, we consume all other things into this self; the more numerous the things we devour, the less we understand them and the less they are accessible to us objectively, but only within this entanglement. Unbelief is flight from oneself, and so the Jews can no longer see through anything in their intellectual game.

To know the Lord, we need to allow him to know us. We must make ourselves totally transparent to him, and this attitude is faith and love combined. His Mother stood thus before his eye in perfect transparency, with the desire to be seen by him to the innermost center. In this, she is the unequaled example of faith and love. She is as we would perhaps like to be before the Lord at the moment of confession: open for his eye and his word. But what we experience in confession from time to time, like the sunbeam of a longing, should become in us the beginning of a permanent attitude. We have made our confession in the sacrament: sin lies behind us and belongs to the past; before us lies only life within the penetrating glance of the Lord, a glance full of love and compassion. We stand within this glance like a little child before its mother and desire that we might never again step outside this glance of the Lord.

THE CLEANSING OF THE TEMPLE

In order to look through us, the Lord needs only his love. We need, in order to allow him to look through us and to see him ourselves in his seeing us, what he gives us: love that is one with faith and hope. Without this triunity, there is no approach to the Lord. It was said before that we cannot know or describe another Thou except in love. This is also true and especially so with regard to our Lord. *He needed no one to bear witness of man.* Yet our life is filled with such witnessing. He needs only his own witness, not ours. What we say, think, or speculate about him does not alter anything in him; he is what he is and is not touched by our witness; he is the Son of God and our Lord. He uses us as servants, and our service consists, not of the description of the Lord, but of the fulfillment of his will. It is the others who need our witness, those who are also called to serve, who are perhaps called to serve him better or in a different way. They need our witness. But it is of use to them only if it is given within a mission from the Lord. A witness that is not service but is only word is no witness. Even this inconspicuous witness the Lord does not need for himself; he makes use of it only insofar as our love for him passes through and is mediated through our love of neighbor. He needs no one to bear witness of another man. He looks through them all.

In knowing what is in every man, he also knows how much each one needs from him, expects and demands from him. There is, however, a great difference between a demanding expectation and an expectant hope. God has no need for me to tell him what I demand and expect from him for myself and for others. But if my neighbor is sick or in distress or in sin, I may pray for him to the Lord. I may not demand or expect the removal of the sin or distress or sickness of my neighbor. But if my expectation is clothed in hope and finds its fulfillment there, everything is as it should be. For hope is rooted in love and one with love. We can recommend others to God, but only in the hope of his love. This hope can even be the certainty of his love. The Lord is able to use such a witness of hope we bear of another. And then, finally, other people, too, can use my witness of another man, if it is borne in the service of faith, hope, and love. As it is possible to bear witness to someone about himself by exhortation and explanation in order to lead him to God, so also one can give him information about others (even if one is obliged to speak about their faults) as long as it is within a mission given by God and part of his service. This will always be so if not only the motivation for giving witness but the content of the information itself, however hidden it may be, is rooted in faith and love and if it is related to the faith and love of the person of whom one gives witness.

NICODEMUS

3:1–2. *Now there was a man of the Pharisees, named Nicodemus, a ruler of the Jews. This man came to Jesus by night and said to him, "Rabbi, we know that you are a teacher come from God; for no one can do these signs that you do, unless God is with him."*

Nicodemus is one of those Jews who dispute about the Lord. He comes at night in order not to cause a stir. He himself wants to enjoy the stir, but he does not want to be seen connected with it in any way. No one is to know that the sensation is making an impression on him. His "faith" consists in not being able to deny the signs of the Lord. But he does not have grace. He recognizes that the Lord comes from God. But this recognition is not a faith insight, only a doctrinal sentence. He poses it like a premise. He presents himself as one informed enough to open the discussion that follows; he wants to lay a foundation that will not at once give way. He does this, not from mere calculation in order to lay a trap for Jesus, but in order to come nearer to the facts. Here the second Jewish trait shows itself: he approaches the matter from an angle acceptable to his partner; he is seemingly generous toward him, gives him an advantage. He is so fond of discussion that he is even prepared to renounce taking the lead in it. He also enjoys finding new and fitting formulations in front of the ear of a listener and by means of this mental achievement to console himself for the inner emptiness and insufficiency he feels. If he is dealing with Catholics, such a man is interested in Catholicism. He is not disinclined to think well of Christ himself. Thus, Nicodemus gives the Lord an advantage: he is prepared to accept the divine origin of his miracles.

3:3. *Jesus answered him, "Truly, truly, I say to you, unless one is born anew, he cannot see the kingdom of God."*

The Kingdom of God is where the sign is; the sign is the proof of the existence of God. But the true recognition of a sign does not consist in accepting intellectually its hypothetical possibility, as Nicodemus does; for this one would have to be born anew. Without this new birth, one cannot be truly touched by a sign. One can see it only from without, as something extraordinary, surpassing human power, but not as what it really is: a revelation of the grace of God; a bit of God's Kingdom on earth. Nicodemus, who has no faith, has no access to this miracle and to the Kingdom of God. He did see the miracle; he cannot deny having seen it; but this seeing did not bring him nearer to God. He addresses the Lord merely from the outside; he does not truly converse with him, for only a believer can enter into communication with the Lord.

3:4. *Nicodemus said to him, "How can a man be born when he is old? Can he enter a second time into his mother's womb and be born?"*

Nicodemus shows his knowledge. He knows that in human life there is only progress forward from child to adult. There is no return or exchange; development occurs in one direction. He is aware of only one life, leading from birth to death. His reply shows, first of all, that he knows (for a Jew always knows). Secondly, that he does not believe, because he attaches no other meaning to the Lord's words than the one he knows already. He wants to remain with his familiar concepts and hear of nothing else. If he were to pass from physical categories to spiritual ones, he would also see in man's spiritual life something that can be developed in a similar way as consequential and logical as the physical life. He could, for example, become a psychologist. He may well begin with this proposition: without God there is no miracle. But in his second sentence he would take back again any possibility for God to work outside the natural laws of development. In his first sentence he says: Without God no extraordinary sign can be given. In the second: It is impossible for the unexpected to happen because I know nothing of it. He makes himself the measure of everything, and so there is no room in his speculation for something exceeding his understanding.

3:5. *Jesus answered, "Truly, truly, I say to you, unless one is born of water and the Spirit, he cannot enter the kingdom of God."*
John the Baptist had already spoken of water: the water of baptism. John had seen the Spirit: the sign and mark of the Lord and so the origin of the sacrament. To be more exact: John had first seen water united with the Lord as a sign of Christ's baptism and then the Lord and the Spirit as a sign of his divine mission. Now the Lord himself speaks of water and Spirit as a sign of a new birth in the Lord, Christian birth.

The birth *from water* is baptism as the entry of a person into the community of Christians. In a double way: as a visible rite carried out with visible water, it signifies entry into the visible Church. As new birth by Mother Church from her water, it is the birth to the community of God's redeemed. It is a real birth in which all that was before is wiped out; it is a new beginning to such a degree that even the birth from one's natural mother is unimportant until the moment when Christ and the Church together give new birth to the child in continuation of Jesus' own birth from the union of Mary the Virgin with the Holy Spirit. Because of this birth of the Lord of the Spirit and the Mother, the Christian is born of the union of Christ and the Church. Christ does not say: unless one is baptized in water and the Holy Spirit. This would be much too weak. Nicodemus could then have seen only a washing in baptism, perhaps a perfecting of Jewish purifications. He would have regarded the child as already being in existence, a child of Christian parents, a potential Christian. He would have seen in baptism only the first initiation, the rite. But a new birth is far more than a rite: it is an absolute new beginning, a creation. A child already existing is not plunged into the purifying waters to receive an accidental washing, but the water flows into the child in order to become a new spring in the child. The fruitfulness of this water is such that it purifies not only from outside but also begins to stream within the child and takes and transforms his life into a new life. One could almost say that the child until then was only a lifeless form, which through water awakens to his own life as a child within the Church.

And the Spirit, the Holy Spirit. So far, the child originates from Christ and the Church: that is the water. Besides this, there is another union of Christ with the Holy Spirit, as it came into being at Christ's baptism. In the mission of the Spirit, the Father announced two things: the Son was signaled out as the one sent by the Father who is to reveal the Father. The Son is also pointed out as Son of God who within the Trinity receives the Spirit from the Father as his own. Insofar as the Spirit descends on the Son, he points to him before all eyes as the one sent by the Father; insofar as he fills him, the trinitarian aspect becomes visible. The Spirit is the property of the Son, and to such a degree that even the earthly life span of the Son can in no wise interrupt or disturb the inner life of God. The first is the manifestation of the Spirit in the manifestation of the Son and belongs to the Incarnation; for human reason it is the cause of faith. The second is within faith itself the manifestation of the Trinity to the believer. Now the Christian is baptized also of the Spirit. Already received into the Church and born within her of water, he is at the same time born of the Spirit. This inaugurates his return to the Father. He passes through Christ and the Church to Christ and the Spirit, and so to the Father.

But he receives the Spirit only through the union of Christ with the Church. What he receives from the Spirit he receives from him as Spirit given by the incarnate Son. Because of the union between Christ and the Church, the Spirit comes only through this channel to the baptized, and only from here the return to the Father is made possible. Since the Father has given the Son to the world, he has given him in such a way that no one can come to the Father except through the Son. This means that the way of the Holy Spirit from the Father to man goes through the incarnate Son. It is true that the Spirit breathes where he will, but he wills to breathe there where the Son has become man: in the Church. His return from the Son to the Father cannot bypass the Incarnation. After passing through the Son, he has a filial quality and so also an ecclesial one. Since his descent on Christ, the Spirit is no longer purely divine, but divine and Christian; he has a christoform and ecclesial dimension. Through giving the Spirit to the Church in his baptism, Christ's return to the Father has begun. Wherever Christ breathes the Spirit, he breathes him toward the Father. In sending the Spirit to the world, he takes the world with him back to the Father. From the very moment when the Son enters the world, he is already on his way back to the Father. This way is straight, even in leading through subjective forsakenness by the Father. Godforsakenness in the Christian sense is never distance from God. Every way in the Church is a way to the Father and, so, entry into the Kingdom of God. In Christ, Spirit and water are a unity, because Christ is one with the Church and with God. Baptism with water is the awakening of the Christian life; the giving of the Spirit inaugurates the mission on the Christian journey. Baptism is the first budding of the Christian life, a new state opening out to something else. Into this opening the Spirit enters to lead to the Father. Baptism is the static condition for the dynamism of the Spirit. A person can be baptized without his own will, but in order to assimilate the Spirit, he must give his consent. The passivity of the person baptized expresses the fact that he is gifted with a new life to which he does not contribute anything; his own activity in the assimilation of the Spirit expresses that he has at once to take up a position to this new life in order to pass it on. The reception of the Holy Spirit is already the seed of the apostolate. Through baptism a duty is laid upon the Christian, and through the Holy Spirit he is introduced to it. For the time being, the child can say Yes through his representative, but later in confirmation he will have to confirm it personally.

3:6. *That which is born of the flesh is flesh, and that which is born of the Spirit is spirit.*

What is born of the flesh is without spirit, because sinful flesh brings forth only sinful flesh. To say flesh is to say sinfulness, so long as we regard only the first half of the verse. We can conceive of men born of sin, continuing in sin, and doing nothing else but living in sin. This would be the case when a man has only the substance of flesh and sin, unable to know anything else, and so used to sin that even the place that should be accorded to spirit is taken by sin—sin to such a degree that everything is related for him to the flesh, is fed and grows by the flesh, and increases flesh. This means, in other words, that he feeds on sin, develops in sin, increases through sin, and thus increases sin. The sin that does not know spirit can be the naked sin of the flesh, but it can also be already a sin against the Spirit. There is also a sin against the Spirit that knows what the Spirit is. This is the greater sin. For more terrible than anything else is the sin in one's own spirit knowing the Spirit of the Lord, receiving the Holy Spirit, and then using what one has received against him. The flesh can play a minor role here, but the sin is without measure because it is born of the spirit against the Spirit. What is born of the flesh and does not know the Spirit is not capable of anything else but remaining in sin on account of the relationship of flesh with sin, which can be sundered only by the Spirit. If the Spirit enters and is accepted, he destroys sin and makes the flesh subordinate to the spirit. Sin against the Spirit would still be possible, but if the Spirit is received in faith, love, and hope, sin against the Spirit is resisted and cannot take root.

So there are several grades of sin: flesh that does not know spirit has no reason to oppose the flesh; it agrees to the sins demanded by the flesh for its own satisfaction, in a kind of belonging to what is below. The sinner knows only the demands of the flesh and nothing of the Spirit, so the sins are lesser ones. Then the Spirit enters and brings insight. This insight enables the sinner to fight his sin. If the Spirit penetrates farther, he will not only expose the sin of the flesh but also reveal his own demands. The sinner receives a new possibility of sinning by remaining deaf to the demands of the Spirit. Finally, he can positively resist them. He not only omits fulfilling the demands of the Spirit but also expressly commits the sin against the Spirit.

What is born of the Spirit is spirit. No man is born of the Spirit alone. Christ alone is born of the Spirit, since he assumed flesh only after the Virgin's spiritual *fiat*. Born of the Spirit and therefore pure, he had no possibility to sin. He assumed flesh out of pure love for fleshly man, and it serves him only for the work of his love for man, who recognizes in him the flesh of a brother and is intended to see through the flesh the Spirit of God. But from now on, earthly man is born of flesh and spirit; he lives in this dualism between flesh and spirit, with the task to make the flesh subject to the spirit. He lives in a struggle and has to strive to overlook the flesh in such a way that the spirit becomes free to accommodate itself to the Spirit of God. God, who created man as flesh and spirit, divides the tasks of man into tasks of the flesh and tasks of the spirit. But the flesh has to stand back more and more, while the demands made on the spirit are ever increasing. Yet the flesh will be the spirit's companion until death and can never be wholly denied. (See 1:14.)

3:7. *Do not marvel that I said to you, "You must be born anew."*
You are astonished, but you should not be. You do not understand because you are not inside. You criticize, but your arguments do not penetrate into my teaching. What makes my teaching comprehensible is contained within it, is its own truth, which can strike only those who live in it. In order to understand what I say, you would have to be within my word. My word can be heard, but it finds an echo only in those who love my Father, hope in him, and believe in him. In this word, the Father and I are one; together we send the Holy Spirit, whose work comes to completion in those who receive us, because we have received them.

"You must be born anew." This means: the flesh and spirit of which you consist must be given to you anew. This can

happen only when you give them back to God in order to receive them anew from him. Only then can the new flesh and spirit be handed over to their Christian destination, in which they move away from sin. When the sinner offers God his flesh and his spirit, God gives both back to him born anew in order to prevent him from wholly falling back into sin. What God gives back to man, he at the same time retains wholly in his possession. And the more completely man yields it to God's power, the more he is surrounded with his grace, and the more this man is separated in himself from his sin. The relapse into sin becomes rarer through the grace that surrounds him and embraces all that is his; as soon as the surrender to God and God's acceptance of it have attained a certain stability, sin can finally disappear. But God always gives back flesh and spirit to the sinner, who is a sinner because he has sinned and could still fall back into sin if grace did not uphold him. This does not mean that an actual inclination to sin must remain, for even this can have been taken away by grace.

3:8. *The wind blows where it wills, and you hear the sound of it, but you do not know where it comes from or where it goes; so it is with every one who is born of the Spirit.*

Within the Trinity, the Spirit blows where he wills. He remains a movement in the direction from Father to Son, from the Father through the Son. He surrounds man, but because he is movement, he does not cease to blow but returns with man to the Father. In relation to man, the Spirit is something threefold. He is, first of all, what fills man and stimulates him in his search for God. He is the one who awakens the longing for God, who gives the happiness to be found in this longing, the joy in God and the taste for God, the desire to be open for God. He is consolation in the sense of consolation and also in the sense of the conscious connaturalization, grace becoming visible and experiential, the awakening of the spiritual senses. All the beauty of the world can awaken or promote this taste for God, can arouse in us the question about God. But all this is still the lower level, the first degree of being in the Spirit. The Spirit is, second, the one who awakens in man the longing for prayer. He is the form of prayer the content of which is love. If love did not have this form, it would rest in itself and be content with itself and cease to be movement toward God, as it always should be. If prayer becomes occupied with man too long, it becomes a good of man, but every love is a good belonging to God. The Spirit animates as breath and wind the direction of every love. For example, the sexual love of the male in intercourse exhausts itself in itself and leaves tedium and disgust behind until the physical balance has returned. Then this act calls for another, which, however, is not an intensification of the first one, and so everything remains unceasingly on the same horizontal level. As soon as the Spirit appears in this fleshly love, however, this latter becomes subordinated to his goals, the physical process becomes secondary, and the main emphasis is lifted to the spiritual: to the love through the woman to the child, to the sacrament, to God. The exhaustion felt before now plays only a subordinate and integrated role.

It is thus with all other works done for our neighbor, which can be called love only when they receive through the Holy Spirit the direction to God and look toward him. The Spirit is, third, the substance of the mission, because he draws from God the mission and the possibility of carrying it out. He leads man to recognize the character of his calling: whether his mission given by God is a personal qualified vocation, to an ecclesial ministry, for example, or a more general one to the Christian life within the framework of the community. The condition for correctly hearing the voice and message of the Spirit is always a desire to be open for God. This openness enables us to hear but does not exclude the possibility of the Spirit's remaining silent with regard to a special mission. It is in every case simply a readiness to receive the mission totally. At the final end, which is God, the guidance of the Spirit is always visible, even when the ways that lead there are not always marked.

You do not know where it comes from or where it goes. When you have opened yourself to the call of God, to the Spirit as substance of the mission, you are ignorant as to what you will hear as answer, from what sphere of the divine mission he will come to you and to which sphere of fulfillment he will lead you. There is a kind of arbitrariness in God's choice. I choose God, but he chooses me in a kind of indiscriminateness as far as I can see. I say, "Whatever you want, Lord." The answer can be quite different from what I expect. This is certain, however: I never place myself at the disposal of God's Spirit without being accepted. But once I have made myself over to his choice, I have no more power over myself except within the choice of God. Henceforth it is he who chooses.

Neither do we know anything beforehand about the power of the Spirit. The Spirit can choose someone who is wholly unprepared. His strength can be overpowering. Someone may be on the defensive against him or not be thinking about him at all; the effect of the Spirit in alighting on him can be absolute and explosive: a total conversion.

So it is with every one who is born of the Spirit. At one time it was Christ alone who was born of the Spirit. Now it is every man who becomes converted. Nothing much is said about this conversion, whether it is sudden and once for all or gradual and by degrees. But every conversion, even a partial one, is birth of the Spirit. A partial conversion is one that does not go so far as to take man totally out of sin.

In this process, we distinguish again between two types of people: the Jew, who tries to analyze the new with his intellect but without the Spirit, and the convert, who gives every room to the Spirit. The first thinks he can get to the bottom of everything with arguments; the second receives the Spirit in the new birth and learns once for all in this event that the Spirit in God by far transcends his human intelligence. He will see some things clearly; others will remain obscure. The main task for his intellect henceforth will be to submit to the Spirit. He wants to be understood and comprehended by the Spirit rather than to understand and comprehend the Spirit himself.

3:9. *Nicodemus said to him, "How can this be?"*

He asks in this way because he has not understood anything at all. He has not made any progress since the beginning of the conversation, for that can take place only in faith. However, he does ask: *"How can this be?"* He does not think it wholly impossible. He would be willing to be open, even though at the moment he still rejects this opening in the polite, noncommittal way that shows his lack of love. He does not break off the conversation but indicates by a question that he wishes to continue it. Though he does not believe, he has not decided for unbelief. He keeps to a false neutrality between the attitudes that he finds sufficient for himself, so that he sees no reason either to surrender or clearly to reject.

His question therefore contains no progress in knowledge of the Lord. Love would be necessary for this. But the eye of love is so occupied with the Lord that it does not and does not want to measure progress, nor is it able to do so. Love wants only growth in love, in service, in intimacy. As soon as degrees and steps in this growth are considered, comparisons are made, and love shrinks away from nothing so much as measuring and counting. We can offer everything to the Lord without telling a lie, but each time when we have learned to know the Lord in a deeper way, this everything becomes transformed into something more all-embracing, which cannot be measured by ourselves but which remains sealed in the secret of the Lord.

3:10. *Jesus answered him, "Are you a teacher of Israel, and yet you do not understand this?"*

With this answer, the Lord once again puts him in his place and leaves the Spirit as an absolute. So far he has shown the questioner that there is a possibility for one born anew to integrate his reason with the Spirit. Now only a negative statement is made: There is something in you that bars you from really listening. With all your intelligence, you will never come to faith. The obstacle in Nicodemus is the absence of love. This vacant place in him is exactly the one that should be filled with the Lord. If Nicodemus were to believe, his emptiness would be filled by the Lord. Nicodemus would also possess the "knowledge" of the truth of the Lord and would not have to ask the Lord, *"How can this be?"*

As *teacher of Israel*, he understands the relationship with God in a purely theoretical way, as a theological statement. He does not live it; he does not surrender to it. The service of truth, however, does not come to an end when understanding reaches its limit but begins only at that moment to be true service in faith. This is hidden from Nicodemus.

3:11. *Truly, truly, I say to you, we speak of what we know, and bear witness to what we have seen; but you do not receive our testimony.*

The Lord speaks of what he knows. He speaks of what he has experienced, of his life in God as well as of his rejection among men. He knows about his earthly destiny; he has a foreknowledge of his whole journey and of his

Passion, and this foreknowledge becomes human experience as he lives through his mission.

What he speaks of is the true knowledge about God and the world; it is true theology. Nicodemus, however, with all his learning, speaks of things he does not know. That is why their language does not meet; they are not speaking of the same realities. It is a theological disputation that is taking place, and so the Lord enters into this situation, which is painful for his love, by speaking objectively and in a scientific way about the truth. He is confronted by a teacher of Israel and cannot and will not appeal simply to his love. When love has to present itself in this objectivity in a cold way as teaching and theology, love suffers. When the Lord or a Christian is not accepted in the proclamation of the gospel, there remains the recourse to prayer. The hurt of the rejection is stilled there. They suffer for the Father's sake because his truth is rejected, but the wound is closed again in God's love. If, however, the recourse to God itself becomes impossible because the Father withdraws in the darkness of the Passion, then they suffer this rejection themselves and experience the vulnerability of love in the cold air of negative objectivity.

The Lord not only speaks of what he knows but also bears witness to what he has seen. Every science rests on ultimate and primary facts of evidence. The truth of theology rests on the ultimate contemplation of Christ, which he does not prove but to which he bears witness. This testimony contains the fullness of all proofs, the heart of his method of witnessing. A disputation is held; different points of view are clarified; but this is immediately brought back to the ultimate positions: the loving contemplation of the Lord and the loving faith or loveless unbelief of man. Speaking about God is possible only in mutual love, therefore, in openness on both sides, in the gratitude of giving and receiving. True theology cannot exist outside of love.

But you do not receive our testimony. The Lord has told them all he has seen, all he knows; he has borne witness to facts. It is a question of things in this world; understanding is possible to man, and Nicodemus as a man should understand them. But men do not understand. They are not open; they lack the capacity of hearing what the Lord is saying. And this is so because they do not want to be open. So they remain closed to his testimony in spite of the explanations he gives them.

3:12. *If I have told you earthly things and you do not believe, how can you believe if I tell you heavenly things?*

The Lord has explained to them how the Spirit comes down from heaven and unites men through himself to the Father. This pouring out of the Spirit and this reception of the Spirit are things that happen here on earth. They are the crowning of human existence, and even though human life is completed by divine life, the divine that comes to touch living man remains of this earth. As long as man lives on earth, he has to fulfill a task here below. There is already now a link between earthly and heavenly things, but this link exists within the earthly insofar as the Christian himself is still on this earth. The Christian remains of this earth particularly because of the task he has to fulfill. Even though his prayer, his apostolate, his self-giving point to the heavenly things, even though they are received from God and go to God, they have their source nevertheless in the spirit of an earthly man, born on this earth. *Earthly* is here understood in a far wider sense than the one meant by the concept *flesh*. This is so because the Lord on his earthly pilgrimage lives through all these earthly things and makes them his own. If the Lord now wants to speak of heavenly things, men will understand even less, because they cannot connect it with what they think of as spirit in the world. In speaking of heavenly things, he will still use earthly parables. He will begin with bodily relationships, will speak of members of the human body, of ordinary everyday things and natural longings. But one sphere he will not address: the whole sphere they call spirit and reason. For what is reasonable in heaven they will see as sheer nonsense. The first thing that changes in their conversion to the heavenly life is the relationship of the spirit to God. The spirit that does not know God will never understand anything about the spirit in God. The distance between them is so great that the spirit without God is absolute darkness, which does not receive the light of the spirit in God. There is no connection here or the possibility of a transition. Both are so different that one who has no faith does not even recognize the language of faith as a language. In spite of this, the Lord says, "I will speak to you of heavenly things."

3:13. *No one has ascended into heaven but he who descended from heaven, the Son of man.*

One would expect that after all these explanations the Lord would break off the conversation. But he cannot do otherwise than draw the man standing before him once more to himself. He does not, however, attract him with cheap and pleasing speeches but confronts him with the most outrageous: no one has ascended except he himself. When did he ascend? Nothing is said about it. Only this is certain: during his earthly life he continues to ascend because he is in touch with the Father up to the moment of his forsakenness on the Cross. He expresses this contact in the language of ascent in order to offer a helpful image to the human need for understanding. He speaks in simplifying images. Though Nicodemus perhaps finds that the Lord expresses himself in an incomprehensible, even ridiculous way, there is no better way of clarifying his relationship with the Father than by the image of ascent. He then also speaks of descent; this is more easily understandable because men are here below. As far as the Son is concerned, there is no changing from above to below. No two planes exist for him, one above the other, between which he would have to ascend and descend. For him it is a horizontal relationship. He always lives on the Father's plane; there is no need for him to ascend there. He is always above, in the most ideal state. But by becoming man on earth without detriment to his heavenly existence, he makes it possible for us who live on the earthly plane to strive toward being where he is: with the Father. In his grace and through his life we are enabled to live in such a way that God can grant us access to the heavenly life, if he so wishes. We cannot ourselves force this access by prayer, meditation, or asceticism. All we can do in this direction is to remove the obstacles that prevent God's building. The building itself, however, and the whole ascent into the heavenly world, is exclusively the action of God.

The Lord, therefore, lives in both spheres at once, which for him are not one above the other but next to one another and in each other, for they are both united in him, penetrating and intersecting each other. It is only we who have to think of God and man as living on two different planes that do not intersect each other. The Son's reality then appears to us as a movement mediating between above and below, as ascent and descent, unifying both planes in this way—or at an angle to each other so that they intersect in him. But in truth, the Son is at the same time on God's plane and on the plane of man, thus bringing both to their perfection. This union, which does not cancel the distinction but, on the contrary, completes it, is for us in the last resort incomprehensible and has to be expressed by the image of movement. In this union of the two planes consists the mystery of the Incarnation of God, of the Immaculate Conception of Mary, and finally the mystery of Christian love as a whole. The mystery of this union is the source of all other mysteries and the wellspring for the reception of these other mysteries by man. In itself, it is not sacramental, but it enfolds all that is sacramental. In the unity of this mystery, the sacraments are not separated and individualized. The consolation of this mystery consists precisely in the fact that beyond the sacraments there is always a superabundance that binds all sacraments into a unity in God, and so also into a unity for man. This unity excludes any speculation about the limit of the effects of a sacrament. If we look back on our life and perhaps state that we were baptized fifty years ago, confirmed twenty years ago, we made our last confession four weeks ago, and went to Communion eight days ago, the question about the time limit of sacramental grace could arise. When do we need to confess again, so that grace follows on grace and no "empty place" is left? How often should we communicate? But all these questions are taken from us through the mystery of Christ embracing all sacraments. Even the question where we stand in all this. This mystery makes timeless grace intersacramental grace. And this grace contains also the possibilities of baptism of desire, spiritual Communion, intentional confession, and every other effect of the sacrament outside its real reception.

3:14–15. *And as Moses lifted up the serpent in the wilderness, so must the Son of man be lifted up, that whoever believes in him may have eternal life.*

The Lord lifted up on the Cross becomes transparent for the Father. We can see the Father only through him and by looking up to him. The Cross is seen here in its height and sublimity, not as the place of suffering. By looking up in faith to the Lord, who is lifted up, our sin is taken away in the same way as the Jews were healed from their sickness by looking up to the serpent. Sin is never effaced by our looking at it; rather, it is effaced by our looking at the purity that draws us from above. This is a simple mystery of faith, still quite independent of the mystery of confession. The contemplation of purity makes us pure with the purity that is a road to love. Purity is never an end in itself. Freedom from sin is never a static place, but a way on which we move, and always away from ourselves: the way from the bite of the serpent to the healing God.

Here also is the place of the saints in the Church and the place of our Lady. In the same way as the Lord is lifted up as Mediator, others also are lifted up in their turn to mediate our being drawn and lifted up through them, because they have already been drawn and lifted higher themselves. When we cannot yet bear the light of God in its power, we are to recognize it at least as reflected in them. Most of the saints mediate something in particular, one idea; they are a ray from the prism, the perfect white light of which is the divine Son. Perhaps one of them contains the exact positive that complements my particular negative. This ministry of the saints is enclosed in the mission of the Son. For no one has ever seen God; the exalted Son and those exalted with him show him to us. In order that we will not be drawn into what is absolutely incomprehensible to us, there is the stage of being lifted up by something finite, which, however, must come to be, never our resting place, but only our passageway. The saints are like small inns on the way; they may refresh us but not keep us back. God hunts with hounds that have to bring the game to him, but the hounds carrying the prey in their mouths may not feed on its blood but must quickly carry the prey to the huntsman.

That whoever believes in him may have eternal life. Faith and eternal life are one and the same reality. Faith is not only faith in eternal life but also the pledge of it. Until now, faith appeared to be a distinct process, linked with love and hope but separate from them. Here it becomes something wholly open, immense, undifferentiated, and unlimited: it is the outlook ahead, the flowing into eternal life. And neither life nor eternity can be limited or categorized; no qualitative description can be made of eternal life; it always exceeds everything by far. No superlative can try to express it, can come near to a positive statement of it. Eternal life is like sparkling rain, like fireworks bursting out in all directions; every effervescence and intensity is its characteristic. Into this faith enters.

3:16. *For God so loved the world that he gave his only-begotten Son, that whoever believes in him should not perish but have eternal life.*

If God were to make a choice between the world and his only Son, he would give preference to the world—the world with all its sin. He would give it preference because it is not yet redeemed. For this unredeemed sinful world, he gives up his only Son. But he gives up his Son so *that whoever believes in him should have eternal life*—everyone, therefore, every single individual. There is something of a contrast, a tension in this: thus he loves the world, and thus he loves every individual. Who is this single individual? One, or one thousand, or a hundred thousand? Each one is for God a kind of embodiment of all, and so he gives to every single one his only Son. The giving of his Son is, therefore, not something done for a world in general or done once and for all. Rather, the giving of the Son once and for all remains in spite of this a multiplication of this sacrifice. In the human birth of the Son, it is not a single going out from the Father that takes place, for this going out is outside of time and beyond time, a constant uninterrupted departure and an ever-new being given, something out of all bounds, not to be compared with our individual, questionable, conditioned, and mediocre reception. This ever-new giving is also the reality behind and beyond all the feasts of the Church's year. This ever-present separation of the Son from the Father takes place so that no individual, even the last of sinners, should on any day live or die without consolation. The Father gave the Son yesterday; he gives him today; perhaps he will give him also tomorrow. But through the bridal relationship between the Church and Christ, we are forced to regard the gift as given and consummated once and forever. There is the Tradition of the Church, which tells me that what happens today did also happen a hundred and a thousand years ago. But this very strength of Tradition forces me today to renounce my sin and look at the exalted Lord. I might speculate that most likely I will not die today; because I know that grace is timeless, I might decide to become converted a month later. But this is not permitted to me because in every today I am the single one for whom the Father has given the Son. Even if I were to die outside the Church: it has already happened for me. From the moment I know that it did happen, I also know that it happened for me. Never, therefore, may I think that the Lord gave himself only for the world in general, for he did it for every single one, and so for me. If I know this, I know that I am meant today, with regard not only to my conversion but also to my mission and apostolate. If the hour of your conversion has not yet come today, it is already today that I must begin to lead you to conversion. As soon as I recognize you in the community as my neighbor, my brother, I am irrevocably obliged to hand you over to God. My obligation to give myself to God absolutely coincides with my mission to you. There is no interval between my readiness in faith and my apostolate in love. God's spontaneous love of today embraces both.

That whoever believes in him should not perish but have eternal life. To perish would mean to die without insight, being delivered over to him whom we did not want to meet, to arrive at the other side with my person as it is, with all the barriers I have erected during my life through sin, through obstinacy, lack of trust, and refusal to surrender. It could also mean to die and take along the dawning of an insight seeking to know God outside of love, a knowledge based on proofs of God's existence. These "proofs" would have allowed us to accept a God but without influence on one's life; the proofs of God's existence do not suffice to bring us into contact with him, for he far exceeds all that can be proved. We can go to absurdity in proofs of God, never coming to an end. The end exists in a leap, a leap of God's love for his creature, exploding its natural reason and creating room for faith in love. There is an interior transition between natural reason and supernatural faith. This transition is forged by the mission of the Son. In the Son we have the proof par excellence, the proof of God's love for us, and so the shell of mere reason is burst open to his love, which streams in. Here to lose oneself and perish ends in grace. It is the grace of the Son, which through his humanity makes eternal life accessible and comprehensible to us, for through the divine in him the meaning of human things has also become understandable to us. Without faith in God and love for the Son, earthly life remains so meaningless for us that to cope with it exhausts and baffles our reason, so that eternal life becomes even more obscure and closed to us. Human life without God begins in loneliness, opens itself to the world, and closes again in death;

it comes from the earth and falls back into the earth; it is a curve that rises and then irrevocably falls down again. This causes its meaninglessness. Life in God rises together with earthly life, but at the moment it reaches its highest point, it opens to the infinite and does not return to earth. The believer does not perish but will have eternal life, in which we shall see God.

3:17. *For God sent the Son into the world, not to condemn the world, but that the world might be saved through him.*

To condemn the world would mean to judge between good and evil in what one has striven for, undertaken, accomplished, and finally in everything one has tried to do for any other aim outside of love. This judgment does not take place because *God sent the Son into the world that the world might be saved through him.* Salvation consists in this: that Christ sees us in the light of his love. To be able to do this, he gives us a share in his love, communicates it to us and clothes us in his love. It is possible that we recognize this love in part, come to meet it, and dare to attempt to do what we do in the name of love. We do it only because we have received this love from him; he gave it to us, for without it, he would find us unlovable and he would have to judge us. The salvation of the world is possible only within love.

3:18. *He who believes in him is not condemned; he who does not believe is condemned already, because he has not believed in the name of the only-begotten Son of God.*

He who believes is not condemned. For faith has its existence in love, and within love this exchange of love between him and us becomes possible. *He who does not believe is condemned already* because he did not have the love to believe, because he had closed himself to love; he would have had the opportunity to meet the Lord, but he declined the offer because his own love appeared more important to him than the Lord's love. He is condemned already, that is, at the very moment when he rejects the Lord's love and decides not to believe. This does not mean that this *condemned already* is final, because the Lord's love is much greater than man's rejection of it; he comes to meet him again and ever begins anew. The Lord continues to send the invitation; there is no limit on his side; eternal rejection is unknown to him.

Because he has not believed in the name of the only-begotten Son of God. For the first time in his Gospel, John makes a restriction. For the first time he demands faith, love, and hope, not only in general, but faith in a definite, absolutely concrete name. So far everything was accommodating. It was a question of God's benevolence and care for man. Now suddenly the name cuts like a sword through everything. God says, because I am the Lord and this is my Son, every comparison and every accommodation comes to an end. That is said to all those who think that they can take or leave as they see fit with a partial, conditional, and superficial faith, without penetrating to its foundation. Faith in the one and only name is suddenly inexorably exacting. For the first time in John, love is not presented as something removing all bounds and reaching to the infinite; it is firmly set into the hard form of obedience.

3:19–20. *And this is the judgment, that the light has come into the world, and men loved darkness rather than light, because their deeds were evil. For every one who does evil hates the light, and does not come to the light, lest his deeds should be exposed.*

This description of judgment appears incredible. Normally judgment seems to be a verdict over a person. Here judgment is made according to one's own preference and love. God does not judge; man judges himself, and in the darkness. This darkness prevents him from recognizing his evil deeds. He does recognize them, however, insofar as he remains in the darkness; he knows that they have need of darkness. He is thankful for the darkness that covers up his deeds. Because of this, he prefers it. The light would show them up and accuse him. So he hates the light. He turns away from God's light so that it may not fall on what he wants to keep for himself in the dark. If I believe, my choice is the Lord's choice; if I do not believe, the Lord makes my choice his own. In this consists judgment.

3:21. *But he who does what is true comes to the light, that it may be clearly seen that his deeds have been wrought in God.*
If a man does what is good, he need not fear the light; his deeds are in the light. He does not desire to place them in the light in order for God to admire them. But he wants God to see everything; he wants that everything should lie open before him; God alone shall measure it. At the moment a man believes in God, he is no longer concerned about the value of his own works. He is conscious only that they are an attempt to act in the name of God according to his will, and he knows himself so bound by it that he has no desire to cover them up before God. He leaves the judgment and use of his deeds to God so that everything may be subject to God's judgment, and he himself will have nothing more to do with his own deeds. God's light is so blinding that when I place my good deeds before him in his light, I see nothing but his light. My deeds that were done in God's grace do not belong to me. Everything I try to do in his name is more *in God* than *done*.

THE FRIEND OF THE BRIDEGROOM

3:22–24. *After this Jesus and his disciples went into the land of Judea; there he remained with them and baptized. John also was baptizing at Aenon near Salim, because there was much water there; and people came and were baptized. For John had not yet been put in prison.*

The discussion with Nicodemus had imperceptibly developed from a conversation with this individual into a dialogue with a wider and widest circle, passed on to us. This is the case with every word of the Lord. When he makes his voice heard, it is never for one individual alone but always for many. That is why none of his conversations is ever interrupted or ended; it goes on and on. In his conversation with Nicodemus, the Lord speaks to the Jews to the present day. The ongoing dialogue must not be understood as the Evangelist's own further development of the Lord's thought or an inclusion of things that he said on another occasion. Certainly, our Lord's words in the Gospel are selected and summarized. But they should not be taken out of their situation and the context in which they were spoken. His speeches are always individualized; the Evangelist gives not generally valid truths but always the substance of a situation.

After his conversation with Nicodemus, the Lord leaves the Pharisee standing and walks on with those who believe. He had first talked to the Jews, then about the way of faith but without attempting to convert. With Nicodemus, he deals in a personal way; he speaks humanly to the man; but to others, to the world, he presents objective truth without desiring to convince or influence anyone. He does not advertise, makes no demands. He speaks in an almost detached way. His truth does not always urge and challenge. For the Lord can wait. He can wait because even his waiting is always a movement of love. His waiting is a form of contemplation, more precisely: of action invisibly present in contemplation. He has no need of using human means of convincing. It is sufficient for him to state the truth. His possibilities are infinite; he has a thousand ways where we have only one. He does not need to moralize to reach his goal. His program is not limited. The number of ways that lead to him are infinite, and he has an infinite number of ways to make himself understood by men.

Now he baptizes. He baptizes with water as John did before him. By himself baptizing, he witnesses to the absolute character of the sacrament. People could otherwise have got the idea of making a distinction between him and the sacrament. They might have been given the impression that it was sufficient to encounter him personally and that the sacrament is a mere substitution made by the Church that can be omitted once the Lord personally meets the soul. By himself baptizing, the Lord shows that no distinction should be made here, that nothing should be sought beyond the sacrament. He fulfills the desire for him through the baptism he gives; baptism of desire is not a substitution for baptism so as to make the latter superfluous. It is the same with all the other sacraments. Our Lord does not withdraw through his personal presence from his ministers the power he has conferred on them once and for all; he does not override his own ecclesial directives. He is not like those commanders who give commands over the heads of their subordinates in order to make their power felt.

John also baptizes. He baptizes because the Lord does not take this power from him in order to exercise it himself. Office remains office. The sacrament is equally valid whether it is the Lord or John who bestows it. It does not depend on the worth of the one who confers it. The Evangelist takes this for granted, for he only says: *There was much water there*. John had chosen this well-watered place; perhaps he had baptized much more than Jesus. He drew at first the greater crowds. But that is wholly inessential. The crowd wants to be baptized in the name of Jesus; it has a vague idea of the meaning of Christ's baptism: access to something greater; and this baptism is now conferred by both.

3:25–26. *Now a discussion arose between John's disciples and a Jew over purifying. And they came to John, and said to him, "Rabbi, he who was with you beyond the Jordan, to whom you bore witness, here he is, baptizing, and all are going to him."*

John still has disciples. He has a kind of religious community around himself. But these disciples, though being disciples of John, have no idea that John is a disciple of the Lord. They have accepted his teaching and his way of baptizing without really understanding that the Lord stands above John. They are the image of those who enthusiastically join an order or ecclesial community and then gradually end up seeing only the exterior appearance of the order. They see only John, and to such a degree that they begin to criticize what the Lord is doing. They no longer see beyond John to the Lord himself. It is their own fault, not that of John, because John has always pointed away from himself. They cling to forms instead of to the Lord—to institutions instead of to his person. They have not fallen away, but that makes their situation even more difficult and perilous. To fall away would be unambiguous sin, but, living as they do, they are living on the edge of sin. This can become a permanent state unless their ears are again opened for the voice of the Lord. They also stand for those who lose themselves in activity, because they neglect contemplation or keep cutting down on it. At the beginning, they looked beyond John and through him to the Lord, but then activism drove them to selective teaching and the chronic state that ends in heresy. Their faith shrinks and becomes lifeless, while a living faith grows and becomes daily more alive. They have the great luck that their founder wants no personality cult and will not suffer it. In this he is the model of the saint.

They are therefore put out about the fact that though John was the first to baptize, the people are now streaming to the Lord himself. At this beginning of heresy, they not only play down the capacity and power of the Lord but also cut the living flowing connections between the Lord and John. They no longer see them. They embody the possibility of a doctrine within the Church's doctrine that in actual fact is already outside the ecclesial teaching because it has become eclectic. They lose sight of the wholeness and absoluteness of the Lord. That is why they draw John's attention to the fact that the Lord is abusing his power. They hope to draw John on their side. John has become an end for them; they no longer see the forerunner. They cannot imagine anything other than that John also would prefer to be the goal rather than the passage. They remind him that he has borne witness to the Lord, thinking this would put the Lord under obligation to remain in a limited position. They imagine that by passing on the power to baptize, the original source from which the sacrament flows has been deprived of its rights. They see the Lord as being bound in his possibilities of communication by the Church he founded. Whereas by himself baptizing the Lord binds himself to the law he made, here it is men who try to limit him by this law. They claim for themselves what belongs to the Lord alone and thus also miss the meaning of the Lord's law.

3:27. *John answered, "No one can receive anything except what is given him from heaven."*

What is given us from heaven is the unity of faith, love, and hope, the unity of sacramental grace, the unity of the teaching of the Church, which is the teaching of the community as well as of the individual. This unity can be given only from heaven, that is, through the unity of the Trinity. For what we receive from the Son cannot come in any way other than from the Son as having received the Spirit from the Father. What we receive from the Father is given us by the Son, who possesses the gifts of the Holy Spirit as the one sent by the Father.

John's reply, therefore, means that he has baptism as something special and unique not from himself; and, too, his disciples have what they have, something special and unique, not from him, but from the Trinity in heaven. He means that every sacrament is ultimately indivisible and comes from the Triune Being of God even when bringing about a special effect and given by one of the Divine Persons in a special way—for example, the Eucharist giving the Son; confirmation, the Spirit. Everything that is sacramental is constantly brought back to the formula "in the name of the Father and the Son and the Holy Spirit". Specialization in favor of one sacrament is forbidden and cannot be endured in the Church. But in our personal prayer life, everything is allowed: I can turn to whom I wish. I am allowed to have preferences. It would be a mistake, however, if, for example, I wanted to go to confession every week but not to Communion, if I were to concentrate on the grace of the sacrament of reconciliation; or if I were to believe that since the Lord forgives my sin also in the Eucharist, I do not need to go to confession. *No one can receive anything* taken out of the unity; it is always the whole that is given from heaven, but a personal color may be given to this unity. We may be attracted more by this or that and even give the impression of a certain eclecticism, but I must know that all these parts are absolutely connected in one unity. Since Mass is a whole and contains and expresses the unity that comes from heaven, the believer must attend the whole of it unless serious reasons demand something else; its effects cannot be divided. Three offertories cannot replace the unity of offertory-Consecration-Communion. As these three are one, so are Father, Son, and Holy Spirit a unity, and the sacraments are a unity in spite of their variety, and each one leads back to the unity of the Church. The sacraments do not know division, as the Lord himself does not: the gift that comes from him has one certain characteristic: it is the whole.

3:28. *You yourselves bear me witness, that I said, I am not the Christ, but I have been sent before him.*

John corrects his disciples. He says: I have strictly limited my role. I have said that I am not the Christ and thereby placed myself in my proper place once and forever. What is true of the unity in the Trinity, in doctrine and the sacraments, in religious orders, in the Eucharist, this is true also for the unity of a community. I am one of the many in the community; with my task and mission, I must remain within the community, and you may not take me and particularize me outside of it.

3:29. *He who has the bride is the bridegroom; the friend of the bridegroom, who stands and hears him, rejoices greatly at the bridegroom's voice; therefore this joy of mine is now full.*

The Church belongs to the Lord. John sees two aspects of the Church. First the form, the hierarchical structure: the Lord, then himself, the disciples of the Lord, his own disciples. Then the content: the sacraments to be given by the Church. He also sees already the community present in which the form of the Church will come to life, in which the system of the Church will be filled through the Lord. The hierarchy embodies the law, the community embodies the capacity to receive, and the Lord gives life and fullness. Bride and Bridegroom together are the life that has been received.

Bride and Bridegroom in their unity are related to each other like a positive to its negative, like convex to concave, like the raised and the hollow part of a matrix. The positive, which is the Bridegroom, remains the same; the negative, the Church, can move away from the Bridegroom and thus produce disharmony between the two parts. Then they no longer fit perfectly together. As soon as that spirit of heresy arises that shows itself in the disciples of John, the Bridegroom no longer finds his fitting place. And then they suspect him because his positive no longer fits into their negative; his place has been moved. Here is the true test for the Church: Do the Church, the parish, the order, the community still present the exact negative for the Bridegroom, or have they moved away from him? For the Bridegroom is ever the same, but one can distort the image presented; one can try to fit something onto him that no longer fully corresponds to him. We are free in the Church to form the margins of the hollow as we like, but the hollow space itself is fixed once forever; nothing may be altered in it. In our personal prayer, we are free; it is possible, for example, to lay greater stress on the liturgy or on the local color of ecclesial customs; feasts can be changed, the life-style of a congregation modified, and this from the smallest local group to the most structured order. But the central reality in all this is the relationship of Bride and Bridegroom, and this cannot be changed. Every opportunity is left open to personal initiative, for human life cannot express itself otherwise than within a certain elastic tension that allows for change. This is true for externals; the central reality of the Church is not elastic. Within this fluctuating and changeable sphere, the community has its part to play in forming the Church, and this is granted her to increase her joy. A model for this is a cathedral that expresses a particular style and taste, a period; limited in its structure, it is timeless in its destiny. This does not prevent the passing centuries from modifying it: the cathedral can be enlarged, newly decorated, etc. The same is true for the altar: around its center, the living Host, the tabernacle is built as symbol of the firm structure of the Church; all round it we find the changeable exterior decorations: different flowers, small or big candles, vestments, images, all this in great variety.

The friend of the bridegroom rejoices greatly at the bridegroom's voice. Why his voice? Because through the voice the different tasks are assigned. The voice is heard by all who are present. It is the invisible but audible channel that unites the Bride with the Bridegroom, ever passing away and yet effective. It unites in such a way that the voice always addresses those who happen to be standing there; it has meant these, and those who come later will no longer hear this particular voice. Those who have heard it will later know that the Bridegroom has passed here. The voice passes by like an exhortation but is enduring like a commitment. To recognize the voice means recognizing the one whose voice it is. It is a characteristic voice in what it is and in what it says.

In this hearing lies joy. Every mission is in its last resort joy giving. Whatever the Lord may say, be it exhortation or encouragement, it always contains joy. For it can never have any other content than that of the very mission of the Lord, who came to save, not to condemn. This is even the perfect joy: not to be Christ, but to be sent before him to bear witness to the light. *This joy* of John *is now full.*

3:30. *He must increase, but I must decrease.*

John says this in the same breath in which he speaks of fullness of joy. He does not say: I must decrease; he must increase. The decrease of man is not the condition for the increase of the Lord. In himself the Lord cannot increase; he is fully grown. But man has to make room for his fullness, the room for which he asks. This room is not an empty space; it is occupied. I, the sinner, occupy this space. And that there may be room for him in me, the sinner—it is the only room he demands—I, representing the community—the community of sinners as of saints—have to decrease so as almost to disappear, and then both things can happen at the same time: the filling of my emptied interior with the Lord, and my exterior witnessing to the Lord. This increase of the Lord in me is the light dispelling the darkness. In this process, the darkness does not escape (sideways); it is consumed by the light. This is the only way in which it makes room for the light. But John does not say: I disappear; he says: I decrease. As a personality, I remain; I am someone, a member of the community who from now on has the characteristic that the Lord lives in him and that he tries to fulfill the task the Lord has given him. God does not bring about death in me; he makes me come to life. So much am I alive that

I say of myself: *he must increase; I must decrease.* This statement is a sign of my being alive in him and my belonging to him. And while professing that I must decrease in favor of the Lord, I become aware of the mission that you also must decrease. But I cannot fulfill a mission I have received from the Lord except by fulfilling it first in myself, that is, creating space for the Lord in myself and so for his mission. I cannot measure this space except that I know that it fills me completely. If it does not fill me completely at once, I must try to create still more room for him. My striving remains a beginning, a start, a constant growth. But his fullness will always be perfect.

3:31. *He who comes from above is above all; he who is of the earth belongs to the earth, and of the earth he speaks.*

We are told: he who comes from above; not: he who is above, God. It is the Son who comes from above. He comes from above, but he comes down to the level where we all find ourselves. And as one who comes from above, he stands above us. What distinguishes him from us cannot be described; it is the indescribable, the Spirit. That the Spirit is above all means that he as the One towers above us, that he is the higher level, the level above us. He has the overall view, while we are "superficial" and see no overall view of anything. We have no overall view of ourselves, much less of others, and still less of him. But his view, his meaning, his towering above us can bring it about that we are touched by him and begin to love, to believe, to comprehend. Though he is so vast as to be spaceless, he is concentration; we, however, though we are individual points, are each by ourselves dispersion. This is a paradox: the Lord in his towering vastness is not something vague but, rather, absolutely concrete, while we, with our limited little interests, who might be regarded as concrete, are at best an openness toward him. The skin is the most extensive part of an apple, but it is only a shell and of the least importance. The core is the most fruitful part of the fruit, the densest center. With the Lord, it is the other way around: what is most extensive is what is most substantial. The Lord's concentration is seen in our dispersion, because always and everywhere he meets every individual in his innermost center and makes him participate in his own meaning and viewing. But the individual who looks massive and could be regarded as the core is no more than the skin. The Lord fills us, looks through us, and in fulfilling us he penetrates through everything and thus fulfills his mission and so also his own meaning. He comes in order to fulfill. He does not come down from heaven merely in order to stand above us, to tower over us. He could have done this as God in heaven. His mission is rather to penetrate everything in the world as the One towering over it. His mission is to enter in, to penetrate. In this way, he becomes personal to us. Were he to remain in heaven above, he might be for us a "highest good"; we could perhaps pray to him from a distance and ask for various things; but it would be somewhat accidental whether we were heard or not. We would not see a real contact between him and us. But by coming down, he reveals himself to us, gives us access to himself. And this universal whole becomes what is most important, not our individual petitions and desires. He meets us personally and allows us to take him personally. This is meant to be understood, not in a mystical or sociological way or as a secret experience, a master-disciple relationship, but as expressing the essence of his revelation as such: it establishes the contact between God and man.

He who is of the earth belongs to the earth, and of the earth he speaks. As long as one belongs to the earth, one's speaking cannot change. One is earthborn and earthbound. But seeing oneself towered over and contacted by the Lord makes one understand the Lord and heaven. Increasingly one will carry the Lord and heaven within oneself and communicate both to others. A personal and real exchange will be established between the Lord (who is surrounded by the saints) and the man on earth who is there now as one sent by the Lord; when the Lord communicates himself to a group—as he does in the Eucharist—and this group receives him, it becomes Christ-bearing. It will bring something of the Kingdom of God into the world. The vitality of this Kingdom derives, not from the person who receives the Eucharist, but from the Lord, who is the Eucharist.

3:31–32. *He who comes from heaven is above all. He bears witness to what he has seen and heard, yet no one receives his testimony.*

He is above all because he bears in himself what he has received in heaven. He comes into the world with new supernatural qualities that, though not in opposition to the qualities of creation, are their pure, sinless, unattainable precondition. Everything earthly has to recognize these preconditions, measure itself against them. That is why he is above all, even when he comes down into the world. His descent is not a descent into sin but a descent of love, and because love is the greatest reality, he remains above all precisely in this descent. In coming from heaven, he *bears witness to what he has seen and heard*, for he keeps here below his intimate connection with God. Everything about him, even the most unimportant everyday occurrence, is related to his life in heaven. It is an expression of the life of God. And this alone already gives him the right to stand above all, the right to be recognized as King of the world, whether we honor him as such or not. He is King even when we do not acknowledge him. For he is King, not as the result of an election, but because of his very being, which is above all. His being is to bear witness to the Father as he has seen and heard him. His witness is not a dry report but has in itself the vividness of the divine: he bears witness to what he has seen and heard by living it out before our eyes. He radiantly brings with him what he has received in heaven and pours this heavenly light out here on earth. His witness is a work of love, *yet no one receives his testimony*. The darkness does not accept the light. If it did, this would mean that the world were about to accept him on his own terms and become part of his living life through the Eucharist. But the world does not want this because it cannot differentiate between life and death. God is seen as death, as the limitation of its own life. The world lives so little in the Spirit that it negates everything that is called spirit. In the language of the spirit, life and death mean the opposite of what they mean in the language of the flesh. In the flesh, everything tends toward death, because he who comes from above comes down to take everything with him to heaven.

3:33. *He who receives his testimony sets his seal to this, that God is true.*

To begin with, he gives testimony to nothing but this: that God is true. For the other qualities, that he is good and that he is love, are perceived less through his word and his testimony than through his being. The Son embodies and reveals all the qualities of the Father, but not all of them at once and in the same way. The first is that we come to hear the Son's message: the Father is true. Only after our accepting this is the Son able to show us in his life that the Father is love. Without the first we would stop with the Son and not look through him to the Father. There is no possibility of being a Christian that would make Christ the goal. He is never a wall or end but always an opening and access to the Father's love. But this access has been made humanly visible for us in human qualities radiantly revealing the Father's love as if light were streaming through a window into our earthly darkness.

3:34. *For he whom God has sent utters the words of God, for it is not by measure that he gives the Spirit.*

God has given his Spirit to the Lord in sending the Spirit. It is the Spirit who enables the Son to express the Father's word. The Spirit remains the living link between Son and Father, moving to and fro. By means of this link, the Son is able to hear the Father exactly as he speaks, in order to proclaim him exactly as he hears him. He does not proclaim the Father's word with his own, the Son's meaning, not with a distinctive color of redemption. He repeats it exactly as it is in God. He constantly brings everything back to the mission and origin in the Father. He does not say: I am the redemption. Especially in the redemption, he leads everything ever more strongly and clearly back to the Father. This is so because *it is without measure* that the Father *gives the Spirit*.

What the Baptist said before about the Spirit in the form of a dove seemed to point to an almost exterior relationship between the Divine Persons. In his final words, he presents the deep interiority of their relationship. It also becomes apparent that the Son was not born of the Father once for all, but that his birth is an eternal event, in which he receives ever new the Father's substance as his own through the Spirit. This eternal birth is mirrored in the earthly birth of the Son. The Father allows the Son to become man by letting the *Spirit* overshadow the virginal Mother without *measure*. Christ was born of Mary. Mary, however, conceived by the Holy Spirit and not by the Father. The Spirit, so to say, exercised the paternal function in the earthly birth of the Son. He acts here as the Father's representative, being that which the Father has sent out. That is why in the human birth the whole light falls on Mary as the virginal Mother; the Father remains in the background. A father becomes father by giving his substance into the mother; at the moment of conception, the son is in the mother; the father is never more separated from his son than he is during the time of pregnancy. But once the son is born from his mother, the father also steps forward out of the background; he now is the father, and his function henceforth is equally clear beside that of the mother. So also in the conception of Christ: the Father remains in the background by allowing the Spirit (who is the mission of the substance and the substance of the mission) to represent him; during the life of Christ, in contrast, it is the Spirit who now remains in the background in order to reveal the Father and exercise the function of making the Father visible. For no one has seen the Father. All have seen the Son. The full and absolute link between the visible Son and the invisible Father is the Holy Spirit, who comes forth from the invisibility of the Father into the light of the visibility of the Son and is seen above him in the likeness of a dove by John.

3:35. *The Father loves the Son, and has given all things into his hand.*

The Father loves the Son not only because he is his Son but also because the Son is the visible witness of the Father and thus contains the Father. He has given all things into his hand: the heavenly and the earthly realities; all that has been destined for the earth from heaven; and all that is destined for heaven from the earth; all he has and all he himself is. All he expects from us, has given to us, and demands back from us. God is so wholly one that he can never be shared out without becoming even more strongly one. He gives in order to take back to himself. What he gives is recognized as coming from him because he demands it back. There is no surer proof that something is a gift from God than the fact that we give it back to him. What he wants from us is only what is good, but what is good comes from God, who alone is good. The Son stands in between God and us; he showers and pours himself out on us by giving us God; however, everything that he gives us is found again in him; he is the unity gathering together everything he has poured out to make it live again in the Father's unity. He is the giver of the Eucharist poured out and the gatherer of the Eucharist received; all the rays of light proceed from him and return to him. That is why the Father loves him. And since God has given everything into his hand, he has above all given him this: to be God. From his own substance he has begotten a Son for himself and given him his divinity. It could be said that he gave his Son his most precious possession: his Son. He gave his Son his greatest gift: to be the Son. He did not give him merely the whole world and thus this high privilege of being the Savior, Redeemer, and possessor of a world; he gave him the still higher gift of this sonship, through which he obliged himself from all eternity to be his Father.

3:36. *He who believes in the Son has eternal life; he who does not obey the Son shall not see life, but the wrath of God rests upon him.*

It is necessary to believe in the Son to have eternal life, not only to believe in the Father. God meets us, so to say, halfway: for it seems easier to us to believe in the visible Son than in the invisible Father. And because God has placed everything into the hand of the Son, we hold the Father in the Son, and faith in the Son already includes faith in the Father. But not to believe in the Son means that God's wrath remains on us. Not the Son's wrath, but the Father's. For God has so loved the Son that he has also entrusted to him our eternal life; but if our eternal life has been placed into his hand, it cannot be wrath that is entrusted to him. Anything that is damnation, temptation, that comes from the devil, cannot have been given into the hand of the Son. He kept the darkness in his own hand and did not communicate it to the Son; for the darkness does not accept the light and the Son. In this way, he has placed the Son on an equal level with man; both stand in the same relationship to the darkness. They cannot dispose of it (with the difference that men succumb to it and the Son can only reject it); they must leave the judging of it to the Father. The Son can prevent a man from falling; but if he falls all the same and turns away from him, the moment can come when he has to hand him over to the Father. The Son is the light that the darkness cannot accept, so he cannot be darkness at the same time. The Father has placed only light in him, that is, only mercy. The Father's mercy consists in the fact that he has placed all that he has into the hand of the Son, and that is his entire love, but not anything that has to do with the darkness and the devil. This does not mean that the Father keeps anything in reserve, for example, the kingdom of darkness. But he places boundaries on the darkness by sending the Son. The Son's mission has a boundary in that absolute darkness that does not accept the light. When the Son passes through hell on Holy Saturday, he does so as the one to whom the Father shows his secret because he no longer keeps it for himself; he is coming to know what is excluded from the light (because of God's wrath against sin as well as his love for mankind).

THE SAMARITAN WOMAN

4:1–3. *Now when the Lord knew that the Pharisees had heard that Jesus was making and baptizing more disciples than John (although Jesus himself did not baptize, but only his disciples), he left Judea and departed again to Galilee.*

The Lord first of all forms his followers into disciples and only then baptizes them. He wants to baptize them when they have reached full awareness of their discipleship. The cleansing sacrament is not to be sprung on them in surprise, but the desire for this cleansing is to be awakened first. Baptism is to be the crowning of their formation to discipleship. It is to be the same as what it is today for the adult convert: closing of the instruction and sealing of the new knowledge. The Lord's instruction was elementary: the disciples had to grasp at least in a summary way his divinity, the Trinity, and the already instituted sacrament. As the Lord himself was living with them, he could fill in all the rest later. The instruction preceding baptism had something hasty and preliminary about it: the disciples had to be made familiar with a minimum of knowledge, which would allow them to become effective themselves at once through preaching and baptizing. Here we meet for the first time the image of Christian mission. The Lord treats the disciples as a missionary does when he passes through a pagan country. He does not instruct them according to the pattern of a Western school. What is important here during the time of initiation is that as many as possible can be baptized after an elementary information.

What is lacking can be filled in later. The disciples know that they have the Lord in their midst and can ask him anything in the future. What they do not know and what will immeasurably advance their full understanding is that they will be witnesses of the Passion: this highest of Christian realities will enlarge their horizon and teach them on a deeper level than any other instruction. And finally, the disciples are meant to exchange with each other and complete among themselves what they have learned. And because he is expecting them to do this, he now allows them to baptize and leaves them to it. It is the first passing on of his mission to the disciples. He shares out his own mission; he now begins the sharing of himself with the world, which he will complete in the Eucharist later on. He leaves them, not in the sense of leaving them alone, but in the sense of giving them a share in his responsibility and in his ministry.

4:4–6. He had to pass through Samaria. So he came to a city of Samaria, called Sychar, near the field that Jacob gave to his son Joseph. Jacob's well was there, and so Jesus, wearied as he was with his journey, sat down beside the well. It was about the sixth hour.

He is weary as we men are weary. He is wearied from his mission. He needs recuperation as we do; he has the same needs that we have. He is not spared the small contradictions and disappointments in life. His recreations are our own: quiet, meditation, prayer. But also bodily recuperation: a celebration, a conversation with friends. But all this, like his taking part in the wedding, is not an interruption of the mission; it is done within the mission. It is about the sixth hour. Nearly always in the Gospel it is the third, sixth, or ninth hour: every hour of the Lord points to God and the Trinity; every hour points to eternity for the Christian.

THE SAMARITAN WOMAN

4:7. *There came a woman of Samaria to draw water. Jesus said to her, "Give me a drink."*

The Lord begins a conversation with this unknown woman. He begins by asking her for a service. When the Lord asks someone for something, it means that he opens himself and gives himself to this person. But the service asked from this woman lies in her everyday world. Again, as at the wedding at Cana, he stands as man in relation to a woman. But this time it is not his Mother but a woman who is a sinner. However, he could equally have asked the woman who was his Mother, *"give me a drink."* For this *give me a drink* means: give it to this man as to your neighbor. You do not know me, but you always know your neighbor because I your God have come to be your brother through my being the Son. If, however, I am your brother, then you are brothers among yourselves and remain so, even when I cease to live visibly among you. Because you are brothers in me, you are brothers to each other. If I ask you for water, I do it as your brother who is thirsty. I ask you for a gift, the smallest one: that from all this water here you give me some. By giving me this gift, you will become enabled to receive what I can give you: the gift of my love. And since I do not take myself what I ask you to give (which would be easy for me to do), I want you to receive the gift while giving and becoming sharer of my giving love.

You will offer me the water from the motive of compassionate love, because you see that I am thirsty. You, O woman, have in you something every woman has, the inclination to love, however slight. You will have shown it to others before me; you will show it to me also. But by giving me this limited love, you create future room in yourself for my great love. I do not ask you to follow me, not even to understand me, not even at this moment to recognize me. I ask at present only this of you, that you render me this slight service. Whoever you are, you are a woman as my Mother was a woman. To be a woman means to have an inborn readiness to love in spite of everything, on whatever level it might be. I am aware of this in my Mother on the highest level and therefore also in you on a very much lower level. The love that I know from my Mother is so great that it allows me to recognize the love in you also. Through my Mother, I know that one can give only what one has. She gave me what she had, life through the Holy Spirit. From you, also, I ask only what you have: a little water to quench my thirst. I ask you for this water such as you have it: with its qualities that do not depend on you and with the joy in giving that is yours. Should the possibilities of this water become enhanced, should the joy in giving that is yours rise above its natural capacity, this will be my gift, not yours. The Lord asks of us no more than we possess. But the water he asks for is pure and untouched by sin, as love in itself is always pure. If he asks more and we need to obtain more, he will obtain it for us. All our gifts to him that exceed pure nature as it is are his gifts, which we return to him. The Church's power is hidden in this pure exchange; she mediates in both directions, loving water as the symbol of the purity of the bestowal in itself and of the cleansing of the gifts we intend to offer to the Lord.

4:8–9. *For his disciples had gone away into the city to buy food. The Samaritan woman said to him, "How is it that you, a Jew, ask a drink of me, a woman of Samaria?" For Jews have no dealings with Samaritans.*

The Lord breaks through the narrow Jewish traditions in order to converse with a woman of Samaria. Thus, he sets the beginning of the Christian mission, which carries the gospel message across all human conventions and barriers. He thus inaugurates the mission to those outside

THE SAMARITAN WOMAN

as well those inside, since Samaria (capital of the independent northern territory) is separate from Judea and yet belongs to the original people of God. The Christian walks all ways to reach outsiders; by virtue of his mission, he can and must seek those who are closed in in their isolation and draw them, not only by visiting foreign peoples, but also by speaking as an individual to individuals.

The woman is astonished that, contrary to custom, the stranger opens a conversation. She is not scandalized by this novelty; rather, a door opens in her to a beginning of that surrender that goes with not understanding. The relationship with the Lord always contains this element of not understanding. We never know what the Lord will do with our surrender, the limits of which as such we perhaps know and are conscious of. However, every beginning of a relationship with the Lord is already our response to a question he asked first. He begins at the very point where we had not expected anything. The relationship right from the beginning exceeds the limits of our understanding. Not only that: the mystery that surrounds the Lord and points to the Trinity cannot be in any way deciphered by our understanding; it remains essentially part of our Christian faith and has to be swallowed by our faith like an unknown medicine contained in a wafer. It remains a mystery and really becomes more of a mystery in the act of faith. This mystery opens a man in such a way that he finally no longer seeks to examine for himself but allows something he can no longer survey to be at work in him.

4:10. *Jesus answered her, "If you knew the gift of God, and who it is that is saying to you, 'Give me a drink,' you would have asked him and he would have given you living water."*

You do not know God, and you do not know his Son. You stand in a place from which it is impossible for you to come closer to me. Not only do you not believe, you reject; you put up a barrier. Not only do you not know God, you do not know his gift. His gift is what you yourself are, for you are God's gift to yourself; you are God's promise to yourself, to other people, to God. His gift to you is also what I am: the eternal Son of the Father, his promise, and the gift to the world that fulfills it. Our relationship is not only beginning at this moment; it has been existing already a long time, because I am your neighbor as you are my neighbor. You did not know this until now. Had you known it, you would have long since asked me for water and I could have given you living water. Those who ask me know me. No one cries to me; no one begs me for something without knowing me. But because you did not know me, you did not ask me for anything; and I had to ask you for something because I know you. Had you asked me, it would mean that you know me and know what I have to give: living water. It is living water because it comes from the Father and is given by me. It is living because it unites in itself the gifts of the Father and the Son and becomes for you entry into and access to eternal life. I myself contain this water, for the water that I give is mine: it is my blood. So it is the same whether you receive my water or myself: everything that comes from the Father leads to the Father and to eternal life.

The living water the Lord here speaks of is everything he has to give: from the empty concept of flowing, cleansing, thirst-quenching water to the water of baptism, to himself, who allows his blood to flow, to the source of the Holy Spirit, who as gift from the Father leads to the river of faith, flowing into the sea of eternal life.

4:11–12. *The woman said to him, "Sir, you have nothing to draw with, and the well is deep; where do you get that living water? Are you greater than our father Jacob, who gave us the well, and drank from it himself, and his sons, and his cattle?"*

The woman raises a double question: From where does this stranger take living water? Is he greater than Jacob? Both questions indicate that she is standing on the threshold between unbelief and faith. On one hand, she needs firm grounds for believing, transmitted facts, a tradition. Her understanding moves within the framework of these limited facts. Within this frame of reference, she cannot see in living water anything but water from a well for the sustenance of earthly life. Her natural sympathy for a fellow man also belongs to this frame of reference as a womanly quality. On the other hand, she is aware in an almost undefinable way that the Lord exceeds this natural framework. In order to understand him, she tries to integrate him into her tradition. She seeks to draw a link with Jacob. She also has her common sense, which tells her that water cannot be drawn from a deep well without a bucket. She is still far removed from true faith. But she has the will to grasp what is beyond her, an inclination to surrender to the mystery that exceeds her narrow world. Willingly she enters into conversation with the Lord and allows herself to be drawn into the movement toward him.

4:13. Jesus said to her, "Every one who drinks of this water will thirst again."

Your water, says the Lord, is the water that quenches earthly thirst; you know no other. Neither do you know any thirst other than this one, which is aroused time and time again. Until now you have not known anything but your daily life, with its ever-recurring needs that remain the same. All your energy has been spent in satisfying these needs. Your daily routine is subject to your daily needs and their satisfaction. So your thought does not rise above these things; you believe only what you see because in everything you look only for what you need and what is useful. *Everyone who drinks of this water that you have will thirst again.* Everyone leading your kind of life will have to go on doing the same. In the same way as your thirst after being satisfied gives way to new thirst, so your past sins call for fresh sins. There is no escape from your life as long as there is no room for me in it; what I ask of you would bring you freedom and life. Only if I bind you will you become free for love. And only when you love me will the chain of your self-seeking be broken and you will be able to love others. Only when you are mine can you belong to others.

4:14. *But whoever drinks of the water that I shall give him will never thirst; the water that I shall give him will become in him a spring of water welling up to eternal life.*

The water that I give contains the absolute, which leaves no room for any other water. The one who drinks it will know no more thirst for other water. Not for mine, either, for this wells up eternally and never exhausts itself. Everyone to whom I give it possesses it always. And this water quenches not only a present need but also a timeless one. In quenching an existing need, it prevents a future one from arising, except the need for more; but I am always present where my water is, for my water and I are one in the Father. We transform you into a being in movement toward God. Not only does my water quench the thirst; it becomes *a spring of water* in yourself. My spring of water, because it comes from me, and your spring of water, because it wells up in you. This spring of water is the living link between me and you, capable of sustaining you, of nourishing others, and of leading you and others *into eternal life.* All that comes from me comes from the

Father, all that passes through me goes to the Father, and through my living water you can take part in this movement. It is movement from eternal life to eternal life, from my eternal life to yours; because it is eternal, it will be the eternal life of all of us in communion. Eternal life is life that ever wells and bubbles up, an image of power and abundance. My water is ever *welling up* to this eternal life, for it is the living link between life here below and life beyond, between God and man.

4:15. *The woman said to him, "Sir, give me this water, that I may not thirst, nor come here to draw."*

The woman is still captured in her world, yet she does not reject the water the Lord offers her. Her initial openness has changed once more; she realizes now that there is something for her to hope for. Her readiness so far has been of a very general kind; it meant no more than not being closed up. Now it has become an expectation of the Lord's water. But the woman is still wholly immersed in what she sees before her eyes and what can be proved, her everyday life, her guilt, the material, fleshly sinful realities, perhaps the little attempts she may have made to escape from it; the small beginnings of real love—all that has made up her life until now together with what she understood the Lord was saying had the same limited format that fits into her horizon. But she grasps one little step forward: that here is someone who makes her an offer such as no one has made her before. Until now she has drawn water from this well, which for a time satisfied human needs. The new thing in this offer is that for the first time it is made once and for all: it is going to satisfy all further longing.

She can visualize this future only in terms of the tomorrow and the day after tomorrow of her daily life. She sees in the promise made by the Lord no more than a lessening of future labor. A wholly earthly labor, having nothing to do with the sins and discontent of her soul. But she sees a gulf opening between herself and the Lord. Until now (in verse 11) she has been aware of what they both have in common. She has summed him up and judged him to be an ordinary man comparable with herself and other men of her acquaintance. Now she sees that he has something more than she herself has. He possesses some unknown superhuman powers. It would be useful and fitting for her also to have a share in these. She desires them in order to put them at the service of her daily needs. Her words *that I may not thirst nor come here to draw* show how much she is still bound into her narrow environment. She says these words, however, with a certain intention: she wants to show how far she has progressed in her understanding, where she stands; she wants to be known by the Lord and led on farther. This also is a truly feminine trait.

She is a woman and as a woman reminds the Lord of his Mother. A woman always sees things from their practical angle. The speculative is not her concern. She turns back to her work and the usefulness of the new water to her world. In this she reminds the Lord of his Mother's womanly qualities. But he also sees what is dark and distorted in this woman and the large and distinct background of her sins. In his Mother, he sees sinlessness. Coming from the Father, she goes back to him through the mediation of the Holy Spirit; she included in her *fiat* the whole journey and the whole being of her Son, so much so that she makes her own all that is his and understands without words what he says and does and where he leads her. He knows himself understood by his Mother; in the Samaritan woman, he sees the spring of understanding cluttered up by sin. He also sees how profusely the spring of his grace should circulate in her, so that every obstacle might be flooded away and the way to God might be laid open in her. He sees in his Mother this freedom toward God: in her, the surrender to the Father is always the same and alive. She and her Son, each according to his mission, walk the way to the Father, the way that will not end in eternal life, but will come to full expansion as eternal life. His Mother is for him the archetype of that purity which comprehends everything by welling up to eternal life like a spring. For the sake of his pure, sinless Mother, he explains this purity to the sinful woman and enters into her world. The way of the sinless woman to God shows him what the way to God of the sinful one must be like.

4:16. *Jesus said to her, "Go, call your husband, and come here."*
He sends her away to fetch the partner in her sin. She is asked to call the one with whom she does what is most of all forbidden to her. She is not to send for him; she is to bring him here herself. Before moving on, the Lord makes the gulf appear that exists between the eternal life he promises her and herself, her own death in sin. Before acting, he makes certain conditions; for in order to be able to receive the light, she has to cast off the darkness in herself. He prepares the way for the light by letting the light shine into her darkness not only in such a way that her sins stand out externally but so that she also interiorly can see and accept her guilt. She cannot go the way his Mother went, who in her *fiat*, opening her entirely to the light, also at once received the whole of the light. Here the conversion has to come in steps: first the light has to fall on her and illumine her darkness from without, make her sin stand out. Only the light can do that. Then she herself has to recognize her sin in quite a different clarity from the one she had before (for until now it mattered little to her), and only then a double movement can take place: that

she tries to cast off her sin and that the light of the Lord powerfully falls into the opening. The small inkling of an understanding that she has just shown when desiring the new water is lifted by the Lord into the spiritual sphere: what she has presented on the earthly level he translates into her relationship to him,

In sending her away to fetch her husband—her sin—and come back to him, the Lord shows how small and minimal the preparation is that is asked of man in order to receive his grace. But there must be a preparation. He looks for a gesture in which the woman admits her sin. He asks her to call the man who is the object of her principal sin. It is not possible to make room for the Lord by beginning with minor matters on the margin. The essential has to be tackled at once. There is no place for human graduations from the lesser to the greater. The Lord demands that the most important be made clear at once. He does not allow a gradual approximation to himself. He wants the big and decisive; he wants the main darkness as contrast to his full light. He suffers no compromise, no accommodation. He is conscious that he himself will have to do the real work. But he respects his brother too much to leave him standing there with side issues. He shows him with all clarity the contradiction between sin and grace. Everything can follow from this first encounter between sin and grace. He expects that soon, very soon, the other will offer his own life to him in answer to his own offer. Man must know from the start that what is meant is totality, not only the whole of sin and of grace but also the whole as regards the exchange of earthly life for heavenly life. The Lord brings us the entire heavenly life through his Incarnation and expects in return that we place at his disposal our entire earthly life for his return to God. We are to leave it to him to make something out of it so that he can lift it into eternal life. From this moment, our earthly life as it remains to us may appear to us perpetually overtaxed, but we must know that it remains in his hand and that with every new demand he comes nearer to us and also places us more at the disposal of others, because he can use for his divine ends the life he has formed. This distribution of the Christian life carried out by the Lord runs parallel to the eucharistic distribution of himself.

4:17a. *The woman answered him, "I have no husband."*

The woman confesses a partial truth. She has understood enough of the Lord that she cannot present him with falsehoods. She wants to speak truthfully but cannot decide for the whole truth. She has nevertheless taken a new step. She comprehends that she cannot receive the gift from the Lord in the state she is in, that this conversation with the Lord obliges her to answer and respond to him. So far the goal of the conversation has been for her a deeper insight, almost a satisfaction of her curiosity, and the winning of an advantage: not to have to return to the well. Her replies so far have been self-centeredly practical. Now she begins to be aware that more is at stake, and she rises to the reply: *"I have no husband."* In saying this, she secretly hopes that there will be no further questions. This half-truth seems sufficient to her. Hesitantly she accepts the Lord's challenge by which he means to confront her with her principal sin. She does it full of expectation but is unconscious of the fact that there is an expectation on his side, too. Her own she takes seriously but thinks that his can be accommodated in narrower limits and can be satisfied with less. She is still self-regarding in respect to the Lord's offer: she intends to gain as much as possible for herself. She sees that a price is asked and tries to keep it as low as possible.

4:17b–18. *Jesus said to her, "You are right in saying, 'I have no husband'; for you have had five husbands, and he whom you now have is not your husband; this you said truly."*

The Lord accepts her half-confession. But being the Lord, he looks right through her, sees her whole previous life, and tells her so. He does it at once and fully. A half-truth is not enough for him, and he does not want her to deceive herself on this point. He wants candor on both sides; he needs a full confession. When he comes with his light, he comes without restriction. A halfway Christianity is no Christianity at all, a halfhearted faith is no faith, a half-confession no confession. The Lord's demand is still the same today: complete confession as condition for his perfect light. So much so that he does not want anyone to make a half-confession or his representatives to be satisfied with such. His severe intervention, "*You have had five husbands*", which is much more than you tell me, this ruthless urging toward the essential, shows that he regards her first confession as only a beginning, a first step where no full stop is possible. He allows no time to pass, either; in every Christian life, and also in the direction of others, there is a certain appropriate speed that must not be lessened, whether it is a big decision or not. In coming to the recognition of the truth of faith, a slower speed may be allowed. But one cannot turn from one's sin slowly and gradually; the intention to leave it wholly behind must be firm. The Lord knows well that in fact this also will be a slow journey, but the sinner's will must be firmly set on a total conversion each time.

So he tells her the whole at once. But in doing so, he does not discourage her. Rather, he encourages: "*This you said truly.*" Here also he is a model for the priest: when something has been confessed, it has been said, and one should not go back on it. The Lord affirms that he has heard the confession and thus lifts the person up. The confessor keeps the lead but should not depress the person; he must always show the possibility of a way ahead.

The Samaritan woman's confession finally shows clearly and vividly the unequal proportion between the capacity for truth of the confessing person and the completion added by the Lord. It is always the same proportion: between man's "good works" and God's grace, between man's love and God's love: it is always the same limited, hardly perceptible openness of man that God needs and wants in order to be able to pour into it his whole fullness. He himself awakens in us the great longing for him; with his graces he entices it from us step by step. He himself creates from our almost nonexistent willingness the proportion he needs. In human love, the lover needs at least a suggestion of agreement in order to arouse love until it reaches consummation. A total frigidity in the partner makes the act of love impossible. To enjoy the quenching of bodily thirst, this thirst must have been proportionately great. In the same way, the Lord not only makes a demand for totality; he also awakens and fulfills us totally.

4:19–20. *The woman said to him, "Sir, I perceive that you are a prophet. Our fathers worshiped on this mountain; and you say that in Jerusalem is the place where men ought to worship."*

You are a prophet, says the woman, and means: you look right through me. You see what I am and what I was. The Lord has made her not the least reproach. He does not ask for this or that. He already knows her. Since he knows the truth already, he has no need to insist on it, to throw light on it from all angles. He has no desire to do this; he is interested only in the light. He himself is the light. For him the light comes first, not the illumination of darkness. And now he has obtained what he was looking for: clarity between himself and the woman. It is this clarity the sacrament of confession demands. The sinner must know himself to lie open and uncovered, with nothing kept hidden; this alone brings about the true effect of this sacrament: the total surrender of oneself to God.

The woman wants to pass on at once and to learn more. She now understands that for her the hour has struck, and the divine enters her life. She feels herself standing on a new level. Sin lies behind her; she is now free to respond to the Lord's demand; she goes immediately to the center by speaking of worship. Having been freed from sin, she has become capable of worship. A new light floods over her; she has never taken notice of it before. She is like one who wants to pray for the first time. But she knows only the letter, the formula, the outer framework, and so she looks for the new and unknown in the old and seemingly familiar. She does not understand—it would be too much all at once—what is the essential in prayer: desire for God, seeking, finding, losing oneself. Time and place still condition her. She has heard about a tradition that promises something new and different, but until now this has not touched her; she has not possessed the key: interior experience. Now she stands at the spot familiar to anyone who has had his first encounter with the Lord, has made his first confession, is rid of his sin, and in his first great readiness surrenders himself to the Lord for further guidance.

4:21. *Jesus said to her, "Woman, believe me, the hour is coming when neither on this mountain nor in Jerusalem will you worship the Father."*

The Lord addresses this soul that is opening up to him as "Woman" (not as "beloved bride"), for to send her farther into his mission remains the mark of the genuineness of his love. An apparent love for her own sake in which the soul could understand herself as the goal of God's love would certainly be a sign of deception.

The hour is coming. It is still coming today; it is always coming. It is the untimely hour that cannot be fitted into any time because it is always coming, expected, and arriving. It lasts longer than the whole of Christian life, not only for the individual, but also for the whole earthly life of the Church. It begins with Christ's birth and ends with the end of the world. It is no nearer now than it was then as far as past and future are concerned. But it is the hour that determines everything for us.

Neither on this mountain nor in Jerusalem will you worship the Father. Neither here nor there, and therefore exactly here and there. Because *worship* does not take place in a particular place, it takes place in every place. As the hour has no beginning or end here on earth, so also the place is not determined or visible on earth. It is the place and hour of expectation. And hour and place lose their meaning, each by itself and both together, because there is room only for worship and meaning only in worship. The Lord does not say: worship will take place in the church or outside of it or that certain Christians, religious, men or women will worship. He says, *you* will worship. You all who are created by the Father. This hour will not be the end of earthly time and the beginning of a new and different time; it will not seal up an ancient source and open a new one. It is the birth of worship itself. It is the hour that is an eternal movement and as such includes everything that is Christian, makes use of all that is existing, is the fulfillment of all that is begun. Everything that has happened before this timeless moment, and every worship that comes before this great worship, is no more than preparation, premonition, and a way toward this worship.

You will worship. This *you* embraces all men who are included in the incarnate Son, who has the Spirit in himself. The Holy Spirit is the Spirit of the worship of the Father; he will be sent to prepare this worship in all men and given to each individual. His distribution corresponds to the distribution of the Son, who also prepares the worship by distributing himself in the Eucharist in such a way that he can gather himself again only through the worship of the Father in each one of us. Worship means for us: ceasing what we are and being what God makes of us, worshipping brothers of the only Son of God. The coming hour will therefore be nothing else but the Word that was at the beginning, through whom all things were made, and who has now also fulfilled himself in the world. This worship contains faith, love, and hope as they have come as living gifts from the Father in order to return to the Father's bosom, bringing home what the Father had separated from himself only for a time: the Son and the Holy Spirit.

4:22. *You worship what you do not know; we worship what we know, for salvation is from the Jews.*

You worship what you do not know. You have a desire in you. Until now you believed that it was your own desire and that it should therefore serve you. And so what it is you worship has come from your sinful desire and helped you only to remain where you were already, in the darkness. You were darkness and lived in darkness, and you denied that there was anything outside that is not darkness. You tried to satisfy your darkness with darkness, and because you had a desire in you, you tried to increase your darkness. You have labored and perhaps suffered, but both your labor and your suffering belonged to the darkness and ended up in darkness; you did not want to leave the darkness because you did not know anything outside of it. And when you made the attempt to worship what was outside the darkness, you worshipped what you did not know or want or recognize. The defectiveness of this your worship was in you and not in me, in you and not in the Father, in you and not in love. It is not possible to worship without faith, love, and hope; these are the foundation of all worship. Your worship remained within your human limitations, seeking God and at the same time rejecting him. It made a pretense of seeking God, but in truth it did not dare to do so out of fear of finding him. Had you truly sought, you would have had to let go of what is yours, and because you did not want this at any price, you deliberately renounced the search. In the possibility of a divine worship in the Holy Spirit and the Son, you saw nothing but its impossibility for you.

We worship what we know. For the Lord comes from the light and returns to the light. If his way passes through darkness, then it is because he has accepted our darkness in order to overcome it with his light and to fulfill his mission: to turn our darkness into the light that he can bring back to God. In his worship lies not only this, that light be added to light, light become one with light, but also this other way, this movement in which our darkness is overcome through his light. The worship of those who believe is always the beginning and end of their mission. Their mission is contained within their worship; their service and help and love are anchored in a mission from God, which in the last resort is a mission to worship. Men work, help, and love, but their working, helping, and loving remain unfruitful as long as they are not part of a mission from God. Every action becomes fruitful through contemplation. Every event within a mission from God comes from him and returns to him and is as event only a passage. If a God-given mission begins with you and takes in another man, this means a movement leading back to God, and you must move together with the one entrusted to you all along the way. You must take him where you find him and must lead him where he cannot go by himself alone. You are God's instrument for leading this person to God, and as such you must be his companion. You enter into the framework of his life in order to expand it into God's framework. Your working leads him to worship while being born from your worship. Worship and work in the name of God form a unity and act together as something of the Lord's water welling up into eternal life.

For salvation is from the Jews. From the Jews we have received the knowledge about what we are to worship, and not only that but also the promise. In this promise that is fulfilled lies our salvation, for we not only beheld the promise but also expected its fulfillment. Through the Jews, we received and took possession of the whole of Tradition, and we know from experience that salvation comes from their midst. For us no doubts exist; unlike them, we are not prisoners of the promise but its redeemed. Whoever remains imprisoned in the promise has not felt its living pulse; he has received it like a sign from which fulfillment is not really to be expected. So when the fulfillment appears, it remains invisible to the Jews. They live enclosed in the promise while missing the moment of transition into the fulfillment, unable to understand, accept, and live through it. This is so because they themselves wanted to adapt their steps to the steps of God; they wanted to comprehend God so fully that no free space was left for the incomprehensible movements of God and of his providence and thus no room, either, for what is comprehensible. The one enters into the other; otherwise, acceptance of God would depend on man's intellectual capacity, and the poor in spirit would be at a disadvantage compared with the clever. Salvation comes from the Jews, but now it is here and no longer bound to the Jews. It remains open also to them, even so much so that it could continue to come from them as salvation accomplished, but under the condition of being accepted by them as salvation in such a way that it can continue to work as a living spring.

4:23. *But the hour is coming, and now is, when the true worshipers will worship the Father in spirit and truth, for such the Father seeks to worship him.*

The hour is coming. This time it is no longer the timeless hour but the historical hour in the life of our Lord. The hour when the promise is made manifest and becomes a fact. For the life began in the Lord and was revealed by him in the Incarnation, and now he fulfills in it what had been prophesied about him. The hour is coming when the Trinity can be recognized as Trinity not only in the spirit but also in reality. The hour is coming when the Church is to be founded in the Lord, at once visible and invisible. The hour is coming when the community comes into being and into life. The hour is coming when the movement from God and back to God reveals itself as faith, love, and hope, not merely through traces left behind from which we could deduce that the Spirit had been there but also in the living seed, which flowers as living fruitfulness out of death and continues to bring forth life (like the blood of the martyrs). In all this, the hour is coming *when the true worshipers will worship the Father in spirit and truth.* These true worshippers are now those who have recognized the Son, all those who have had faith enough to enable the Lord to enlarge it. The stronger their faith is, the greater becomes its capacity to be enlarged. The greater their love, the more limitless its capacity for expansion and the more hope increases, the more secure and certain, well-founded, is its transition to eternal life. Faith, love, and hope are the anticipation, the foundation, and the beginning of eternal life. And as Father, Son, and Spirit have always been one in the fullness of eternity, so faith, love, and hope are the unity that gives to men access to eternal life and brings them the fulfillment of the Father's promise. The true worshippers are therefore those who experience this fulfillment of the promise and are enabled to worship with everything the Father has awakened in them through the Son. Theirs is not a partial worship; it is a complete worship in the human sphere because this sphere has been enlarged through the Lord.

These worshippers will worship the Father *in spirit and in truth*. Spirit and truth cannot be separated; they belong together because they have their common root in God. The spirit was created to receive the truth and live by it; it is the truth that gives its full power, its meaning to the spirit. The worship of the Father can take place only in spirit, for the spirit alone of the true worshippers needs no proofs. It is not bounded in by this life but is open to every enlargement, every possibility, as long as it comes from the Father. The worship takes place in truth because the true worshippers know no doubts; the coming of the Son, though they have scarcely comprehended it, is already sufficient to awaken their entire longing for God, the God who gave the promise and from whom they now receive while worshipping the fulfillment that is being accomplished in the Son. They recognized the Father's love in his coming and his works, and through the Son the Father's truth became their own truth. In the love they have received from the Father through the Son, in the demand it makes on them to be distributed in them and through them outside their own persons—they recognize that this love, even though it has become their own, has to remain a wholly divine love. Worship is thus for them an obligation at the same time as it is a fulfillment; not for their own sakes do they worship; rather, they want to fulfill the Father's demand because the Father seeks and calls for such worshippers in whom the brightly shining light is his light, the love that desires to give itself is his love, and the longing for immolation wants to be the thanksgiving for his immolation.

Worship is always a response to a question that comes from God. The true worshippers who worship in spirit and in truth do not appear before God in their own right; they come as people responding to the Father's seeking. The Father *seeks them* because he needs them. He needs them for his glorification in the Son and for the glorification of the Son in him; he needs them to show that both glorifications have become one single one in the Spirit. That is why he seeks them. He uses, not just any people who have offered themselves, but those whom he himself has chosen for this service and to whom he has given all that they need for this, which is to be able to worship in spirit and in truth. This spirit and truth come from him; he invests the worshippers with them as his personal gift so that they may come to life in them and develop into worship. They receive the Spirit of the Father, who proceeds from the Father and returns to him. But no Spirit of the Father can henceforth come to men, transform them, and be offered back to the Father without the help of the incarnate Son. When seeking true worshippers, the Father therefore seeks them where the Son is; he seeks in them not only his own Spirit and his own Truth but also the fruit his gift bears in the Son. From now on, there will no longer be an immediate relationship between the soul and

God without the incarnate Son being part of it. Even the most interior worship, the most hidden prayer in which the soul turns to God or is lifted up into this mystery by God, takes place only through the Son. The Father can speak a divine word to the world, but the echo that returns cannot be other than an echo in the Son. It is a Christian word that comes back to him. The Father, the Son, and the true worshipper form an inseparable triad. As the man calls for the woman in order to know himself in her, to encounter himself in this other image as in a true mirror, so the Father does not call for himself; he does not want to hear his own voice echo back to him from the world; he calls for the Son. And as the full answer of the woman lies not only in her surrender but also in the fruit of her body, which she gives to the man, so also the Son answers the Father by placing before him the worshipper in spirit and truth. The man is no longer concerned with what he has given as seed; even so, the Father does not seek his own question; what he seeks is the living answer, the fruit that has grown from it.

4:24. *God is spirit, and those who worship him must worship in spirit and truth.*

There is no other worship of God except worship in the spirit. But God gave not only spiritual gifts to man. The gifts of the body also come from him: nourishment and clothing and whatever else our earthly life requires. The Father gave all these to us, not in order to take them away again, but rather that we might use them in such a way that they may sustain and foster our spiritual life in true subordination to the gifts of the spirit. He created the goods of our senses, imagination, and emotions; he has given us the key to the realm of beauty: in nature, in culture, in every form of play and art, and he did not begrudge us this beauty but poured it out in superabundance. He bestowed on this world of the senses a kind of magnificent largesse and infinitude, and on us the capacity of being enraptured and inebriated by its beauty. But these gifts, too, are meant to nourish the soul's true contemplation, to lead us to worship in spirit and in truth. They are given to us to keep our spirit alive and lead it upward and ennoble it, to awaken and feed in us the longing for God. A person who really believes in and loves God will always and everywhere see in these gifts an image of the life of grace in God. The blissful longing that a landscape or a work of art can arouse in him gives him wings and makes him soar upward to still greater and larger and more infinite longing. His senses, which remain bound to his bodily existence and follow organic laws, open new windows to the world beyond and become perfected only through this opening. In the always imperfect listening to an earthly music, the true believer becomes aware in himself of a longing for the melody that will be heard only in heaven. Even the full bodily act of consummation between lovers, if it is to be Christian, must give a foretaste of heavenly love, which will be infinitely more fulfilling than anything that can be called love here on earth. Those savoring beauty and lovers stand in their own way if they are merely enjoying. The enjoyment to which they surrender contains an infinite promise, but they know that it is impossible to lead this promise to its fulfillment in this life. It is a part of earthly beauty that it is a mirrored image and faint reflection of paradisical beauty. The world of the senses is a preliminary step toward the spirit. It is not denied to us; rather, it is a gift from God that we might fulfill ourselves in and through it toward the spirit. It is the fulfillment of our being in the state of becoming. Everything that in this earthly life is capable of nourishing our longing reaches us, not without our senses, but in view of the spirit. We behold the beauty of this world and, in doing so, lift up our eyes to the beauty of the spirit. This is possible for us only if our spirit is already on its way to God, open for worship in spirit and in truth. Then contemplation in the spirit can experience an enlargement through our senses' contemplation of all that is true, good, and beautiful. These goods in themselves have their fulfillment in the spirit. They are not neatly separated from the spirit like the basement from the first floor. Already on their sense level, they bear a spiritual form. They are capable of taking their place in the ascending order of the ever greater. Enjoyed in the spirit, they do not satiate but, rather, foster the true hunger and thirst of the spirit for God. But apart from God, they distract us from God. We then try to find our enjoyment in them and seek to exclude from this enjoyment anything that could remind us of the limitations of nature and the world; the things of beauty then become a kind of artificial prison, a closed aesthetic paradise, which, however, ends up by being no more than an expression of our sin and despair. The effects the good things of the senses produce on a man depend on his disposition. If he is closed up in himself, they will close him still further. If he is open to God in faith, love, and hope, they will nourish and enrich the vitality of his life in God.

God grants us recreation on the sense level as a prolongation of the contemplation of the spirit. He does not begrudge us these good pleasures of the senses, the beauty of the world and of art, so that through all this the material and earthly world also may have a share in the worship in spirit and in truth. To reject these goods would be open ingratitude and a rejection of a part of this worship itself. Without them, our active life would soon become empty activity. We should not take it to be a law of perfection simply to renounce the enrichment of our spiritual contemplation through these goods. These acts of contemplation also arise from the gifts of God and lead to perfect worship in spirit and in truth, and not least there is here also for us an approach to our neighbor. The recreation that enriches us ever anew gives us also the contacts that our mission needs; in enjoyment together, mutual love also is nourished and enlarged, and each one, rejoicing in the other's joy, grows in gratitude to God. Christian renunciation is not suspicious of beauty and its enjoyment; the greatness of the Creator is not opposed to the beauty of his creatures. True renunciation means not to indulge in unrestrained and selfish enjoyment of God's gifts but to give them back to the Creator while enjoying them.

Joy is necessary to human life. It is even more necessary the more differentiated a man's mission is. He needs joy to be able to fulfill his task, for in him as God's messenger, love should be attractive, lovable, and captivating. Only one who himself has been enraptured can enrapture others with the love of God. In the gifts of God and the enjoyment they give, the ways and missions of men touch each other. The gifts and the missions are different but complement each other in the same way as the quarters of an orange all touch the common center and complement each other, forming one fruit. This rounded, undivided fruit is the love of God rising from the world, his worship in spirit and in truth.

4:25. *The woman said to him, "I know that Messiah is coming (he who is called Christ); when he comes, he will show us all things."*

In this knowledge, the woman summarizes the Jewish tradition and puts an end to it. And at the same time, she also summarizes her confession by declaring herself ready for the Lord's coming. He will show us all things. He will bring the final fulfillment. She is open to it. So she comes from this conversation with soul enlarged and more ready for God than she has ever been. But she is still moving in her own sphere, and she could never discover of herself that Christ is the one expected. She needs somebody to tell her. It is the Lord who does it, but it could be any Christian, any lover—not the kind of lover she has known before, but anyone who announces the new love.

The Lord's Mother was able to receive all truth without a lot of explanations because she was already in possession of faith and love and in her no sin barred the way. The Samaritan woman, in contrast, stood in need of being emptied bit by bit until she was capable of hearing her own personal annunciation. Now she has arrived this far. After a life of sin, but washed clean through the presence of the Lord, through the general absolution that he gave her after hearing her confession, through the recognition of being surrounded by the Lord's knowing as by a larger space transcending her own narrow one, in which her own darkness has been changed into his light and room has at last been made for the decisive word of the Lord.

4:26. Jesus said to her, "I who speak to you am he."

This word of the Lord completes her conversion. She receives from him faith in his divinity, and so he opens to her his own infinite horizon. In faith, the gulf between God and Christ, between Father and Son, is bridged for her. Through the action of the Holy Spirit, she understands their unity. Whenever Christian faith takes possession of a person, the Trinity becomes a unity for him. For at this moment he begins to share in eternal life, which is no other than the unity of the three Divine Persons. Knowledge can reach the three Persons as such, but faith transcending knowledge grasps their living oneness. It is love that leads beyond knowledge in faith, and it is love that unites the three Persons. From the moment a man believes, everything he receives is given in the name of the Father and the Son and the Holy Spirit.

4:27. *Just then his disciples came. They marveled that he was talking with a woman, but none said, "What do you wish?" or, "Why are you talking with her?"*

The disciples, who look after the bodily needs, return to the Lord, who looks after the spiritual ones. The Lord does not despise the body; it is the Father's creation, which he gratefully recognizes and accepts. He is the model showing us how we are to understand and live the enjoyment of the good and beautiful things of earth. According to the spirit, he is in the Father, but according to the flesh, he is a man among other men, exteriorly no different from them. He has the same habits and physical needs as they have; openly and unashamed, he makes use of everything he needs for sustaining his life; this aspect even receives the emphasis during the whole of his earthly life. He takes part in people's joys, feasts, weddings. He has personal friends; he distributes bread and fish in abundance; he eats and sleeps. He gives the best wine, and wherever he gives he does so with superabundance. He knows the lavish bountifulness of earthly goods, not because he himself is a squanderer, but in order to allow as many as possible to share in them. But material superabundance becomes for him always a way to and an image of the spiritual, a pointer to the superabundance of his Father. *The disciples marveled that he was talking with a woman.* They marvel first of all because so far they have not seen a place for woman in the life of the Church. Everything has taken place between the Lord and men. They know little of the Lord's Mother, and they know her only as mother. They also see in woman, especially an unexpected one, a potential connection with sin and temptation. In spite of this, they ask no questions and have an intuition that something new is afoot. They are aware of the content of the Lord's conversations and that they all lead to the Father. They realize that women also will find salvation. But at the moment, not as yet seeing a Kingdom of God, it appears to them too precipitate. They do not see a possibility of conversion for a public sinner. They can visualize a relationship with God, with the Trinity, only in orderly circumstances. This sudden step from flourishing sin to grace exceeds their powers of imagination. Confession is still unknown to them. They can see only baptism as a means of forgiveness of sin and hope to be enabled to remain in this grace. That there could be a second sacrament for the forgiveness of sin has not occurred to them because they do not yet know the vitality of the Christian life and the necessity that exists for their sin to be vanquished again and again.

4:28–29. *So the woman left her water jar, and went away into the city, and said to the people, "Come, see a man who told me all that I ever did. Can this be the Christ?"*

She leaves the jar behind. She does not carry the water home; she is wholly overwhelmed by the Lord's message. The earthly interests have disappeared for her at this moment; the heavenly things have taken over. She does not yet understand that these have their place on different levels. Perhaps she really does believe that henceforth she no longer needs earthly water. She represents the image of those who have caught their first glimpse of the whole and imagine that in the future it will so fill their lives that even their habitual occupations will cease. They see the absolute of Christianity, but not yet its application. They are expecting pure contemplation without having been called to it. This woman is in a normal phase of Christian development, which, however, is only a passage. She will later come to see that to believe does not mean for her the abolishment of daily duties. The readiness to give herself that has been awakened in her will of necessity be expressed in forms of everyday life. There lies a danger hidden in this time of transition: it could be expected that the grace of conversion received will automatically transform the whole of one's exterior life, that grace has been given once and for all and no self-denial or sacrifice, no further development in daily living is necessary. Many fall away when this miracle does not take place. For grace is much easier to accept when it comes as an outstanding event rather than as a constant and continuous influx.

But at once it becomes clear that the Samaritan woman is in possession of what will preserve her from this danger: the apostolic impulse. She must pass on the truth she has received. A spontaneous urge compels her. *She went into the city and said to the people, "Come, see a man who told me all that I ever did."* She is compelled to do this at once, even before she is very clear herself about the Lord and about how it could have happened to her in the first place to encounter the Messiah.

Can this be the Christ? Her faith is still groping and unsure. So she puts the question about his identity a second time. She still believes herself in need of more proofs. He said to her, *"I am he."* However, she believes that she needs to ground her faith on the confirmation of her own experience—since the Lord told her everything about herself—rather than on the enormity of the claim he makes for himself. She prefers to build her faith more on seeing for herself than on hearing and accepting the word she has heard.

4:30. *They went out of the city and were coming to him.*
The people immediately respond by walking toward him. They believe what the woman says on account of her personal experience. They recognize without much ado that something real has happened. This shows the power of grace, which can radiate and act through anything, even an imperfect medium. For ultimately, these people go to the Lord much less from curiosity than from being drawn by his grace.

4:31. *Meanwhile the disciples begged him, saying, "Rabbi, eat."*
The disciples have brought food and urge him to eat immediately. The woman, however, left the latter behind and believes that she no longer needs it. The disciples awkwardly urge the Lord to satisfy his hunger, while the woman has forgotten to offer him the water he asked her for. The difference between a man's and a woman's faith is seen here. The men followed him at once without hesitation, but they expect the Lord to provide a certain security of lifestyle, with food and drink. Their conversion occurred without sensation, their faith is calm and genuine, but they need to be trained gradually to sacrifice and renunciation. The woman, in contrast, has been lifted into the divine life from the midst of her sin and darkness; her faith is a leap into eternal life, and she desires to leave everything behind that belongs to her former life, all the more so since she now recognizes the connection between earthly need and sin. The men arrived more swiftly to steadfast faith; they have been with the Lord for some time, but they need from time to time new stimulation and encouragement, even certain basic securities in order to remain faithful. They do not leap over any step. The woman's faith, however, is a single act once and for all; she surrenders even before she has fully understood and

while only imperfectly grasping the relationship between the earthly and the heavenly. She believes the water of eternal life to be sufficient for her, making all earthly water henceforth superfluous. Herein lies the strength but also the vulnerability of her faith. It is less secure; that is its beauty and its danger.

4:32. *But he said to them, "I have food to eat of which you do not know."*

The Lord's food lies hidden in his mystery. It is invisible to men, for outward appearances cannot betray it. They do not see its presence or how he feeds on it. No obvious effect gives them a clue about where to look for this unknown food. The food he speaks of is contained in the mystery of his Person. It is the first time that he mentions it, and he points it out as something unknown to them. It contains something that is hidden and has to do with his relationship with the Father and perhaps is its essence. This relationship is unknown to men. They keep believing that if he has come from the Father, then he has brought with him nothing more than memories, perhaps also the possibility of prayer. They imagine this prayer to be like theirs, only more perfect, more frequent, more intense. They cannot visualize that even in his earthly life among them he remains totally in the Father. This blank space in their knowledge is where the secret of his food lies hidden, his living relationship to his Father. For his essential nature is to remain in the Father and be nourished by him in this invisible remaining. Without this food, he would at once cease to live. It is of such elementary necessity to him that he does not even speak of it. Men have physical needs that are taken for granted, and no one expressly mentions them; so the Lord also has spiritual needs belonging to his nature that he does not mention because they are mysteries of the divine intimacy. A mother does not constantly remind her grownup son of the fact that she nourished him with her milk. Neither does the Son speak of the fact that the Father constantly nourishes him.

4:33. *So the disciples said to one another, "Has any one brought him food?"*

The disciples show by this question that they have understood nothing. They are perplexed, for they have provided this food at his command, but now he is not interested and indicates another kind of food. They seek an explanation but can think only of possibilities within their own human sphere. Their faith moves within a small everyday horizon; they regard him as a kind of higher and ideal man with whom they might catch up through their best endeavor and who himself is still striving, not living in possession of his fulfillment. So they come to the conclusion that someone has been here and given him food. That is the beginning of a rumor. Rumor and gossip keep recurring in the Gospel and are the main content of imperfect faith and unbelief. What cannot be understood must yet be accounted for, and this most often cannot be done without presuming and inventing unknown human causes.

4:34. *Jesus said to them, "My food is to do the will of him who sent me, and to accomplish his work."*

The Lord does not lose patience, though their reasoning is so earthly. But he cuts off the gossip at its root. He gives a fully sufficient answer; he declares that he is nourished by the Father's will. He accomplishes this will within his mission, in the constant movement between Father and Son, between Son and Father. This movement does not exhaust itself; it is always fruitful for both Father and Son and nourishes the Son by mediating with every new commission from the Father the strength and possibility of its accomplishment. In the Son's obedience to the Father, in his desire to do the Father's will, lies a grace, an enabling power that constantly increases as the task is being fulfilled. Whatever comes from God is meted out so abundantly that it gives more strength than is needed for that particular mission, a grace overflowing the limits of the task. The grace that is given makes the accomplishment of the task, of course, possible and fulfills it, yet the superabundance that remains becomes the main issue: in the strength of this superabundance, in the momentum that surpasses it, the Son fulfills the limited task without thinking of measure and limit. He has been set in an infinite motion, and in this he goes his way step by step without counting or measuring each step.

This is the nourishment of grace by which he lives. The Samaritan woman also thinks that she should henceforth live by grace alone. But the mission and grace are quite different for each. The Lord actually has it in its fullness; the woman only believes she has it. He comes from contemplation and returns there through action. The woman flees from action to contemplation without having been called to this.

Among men it is true that the different calls from God are manifold. They are each quite different, and there is no possibility of our measuring or comparing them against each other. But it is certain that every call that comes from God guarantees the spiritual nourishment that is required in such a way that the one called need not worry about the earthly food. The strength offered increases with the vocation; the more direct and exclusive the latter, the more strength is placed at the disposal of the one called. Another person who has not received this call would not be able to accomplish it. The fact that one comes to a borderline where one feels overtaxed is actually the sign that the call is genuine. God expects of those he calls that they use only a minimum of the strength offered for their own nourishment in order to put the rest at the disposal of those others whom every mission ultimately addresses. God does his work by distributing vocations and using various instruments, for, in this sharing, the movement toward him comes into being. This sharing is a sign of fruitfulness; life and growth are inaugurated. The food the individual is offered is always personal, differentiated, but this differentiation is uniquely at the service of a richer and more vital unity to which all missions tend. At the center of the vocation, it is the Lord who is at work, but the man who works for him is not farther away from God through this mediation of the Lord. What the Lord mediates is precisely the immediacy between man and God. The same is true for others who are called, the saints: all the relations of the workers, the priests, the community, the Church with God do not lose their directness through Christ's mediation and that of the saints but become more alive and vibrant. No one has ever seen God, but he can become concrete in those he has called. The piety of so-called little people, which is directed to God but clothes itself in devotions to a favorite saint or in a particular devotional practice, should not be seen as misdirected because it uses a mediator. But the more one who has been called is seized by the differentiated and himself differentiating Holy Spirit, the more unified his relationship to God becomes: the tasks here below are more differentiated, but the relationship to the beyond becomes more simple and immediate.

4:35–38. *"Do you not say, 'There are yet four months, then comes the harvest'? I tell you, lift up your eyes, and see how the fields are already white for harvest. He who reaps receives wages, and gathers fruit for eternal life, so that sower and reaper may rejoice together. For here the saying holds true, 'One sows and another reaps.' I sent you to reap that for which you did not labor; others have labored, and you have entered into their labor."*

You say, *"There are yet four months, then comes the harvest."* You have your proverbs, and you talk in many other earthbound ways. And it is difficult for you to relate your daily duties and cares to the duties and cares entrusted to you in the name of the Father. But you are meant to find comparisons, images, and relationships between earthly reality and the Kingdom of God. Because your tasks as apostles among men should be more differentiated, you have to learn how to draw from everything parables that point to the ultimate, to God, in order to build for people a road to eternity from their ordinary lives. The fields do not ripen all of a sudden; they already show signs of the coming harvest long before. Nature allows us to see the preparations for the harvest in advance. If this is true for the fields, how much more is it true for the harvest of the Father, who wants to reap human souls. The various phases of the differentiated work of sowing until the end of the harvest all unite in one great movement toward him who reaps. The reaper receives the fruit and reward of the labor. But he does not forget the individual who did the sowing for him. The work was accomplished at different times and with differing success as far as can be judged by exterior standards. But it was all part of the same work in the one field of the Father. The Father does not forget the sower; he recognizes his work insofar as it is done in his name, for the field is his. While reaping, he also remembers the sower so that the latter may see the interrelations and be encouraged in his mission and see in the Father's harvest his own call to new sowing. Once a mission is fulfilled, it already contains a new mission. Every seed points beyond the immediate harvest and to a future sowing. Priestly ministry, religious life, lay apostolate: nothing is self-contained; today's believing and hoping contain in seed the whole future: it is only in the future that today's love will become manifest.

What the reaper gathers, he gathers as fruit *for eternal life*. The whole harvest is eternal. It is unthinkable that something done as a task from the Father should not be destined for eternal life. What is sown may be gathered immediately, or a thousand other tasks may come between sowing and reaping: the sign of authentication of the work is its orientation to eternal life. All fruitful work tends to the Father, however indirect and isolated it may appear in the world. As long as it is done within the mission, it is fruitful for eternal life. The hour of harvest will prove this, and the joy of the worker will be in this recognition. It is in itself already a great reward that the *sower and reaper may rejoice together* without in the least remembering the past labor. The vision of the harvest is eternal joy; it is the great harvest festival of the world.

Sowing and reaping are done in the Father's name, but the harvest itself belongs to the Father alone, because the sowing was done in his name. He allotted the task and sent the Word to bring home all men. He is the goal of the maturation of the world, and because he is the goal, he is also the beginning. But it is nevertheless true when the Lord says that he has sown and *sent* the disciples *to reap*. He sowed the seed because he himself is the living seed of the Father. And the disciples reap because no man can make a beginning that is not first made by God. Human work is always already a harvest God has sown beforehand. All human sowing and reaping are contained and held within the all-embracing sowing and reaping of God.

The human worker is inserted between God's beginning and ending. His work can be fruitful only when it understands itself as work within this comprehensive surpassing work of God. Man has no overall view of the sowing or reaping; this perspective he has to entrust to the Lord in faith, love, and hope. Among the workers there can be one who fails; this will happen if one tries to sow and reap for oneself. He does not insert himself into the order of the Church and of Tradition and brings about a schism. Then his work becomes unfruitful for eternal life. Good and bad work is judged by the criterion whether it is done within or outside of the Father's commission. The special task of each individual is enveloped in faith and love, which is the environment that links the particular with the entire work. A person living by faith and love is indifferent to when and how he is going to be used. But in all Christian work there remains an element of uncertainty because of the lack of an overall view. Rain, drought, hailstones can threaten the harvest. As in every human work there is an element of risk (for it could fail), so also the work in the Father's harvest often not only is hard but also arouses fear. This fear is a sign that faith, love, and hope are alive. Seen from the outside, these appear complete and reasonable, but within themselves they are full of contention because it is development and growth into the infinite. Ultimately, they obey only the law of God, which is always an explosive force. Not only the result of the work, the harvest, remains beyond calculation, but also the work itself.

Since the individual usually is only one member in the chain of workers, he must be capable of entering *into the labor* of others in order to complete a work inaugurated in the name of God but according to another method and style. Of course, this does not mean that work should be splintered up by entrusting an organic plan to different people in succession without a serious reason—the unique talent of a worker should also be respected in the service of a work of God. In every organization, however much in flux, there should be certain periods of rest; time must be allowed for a work to insert itself organically into the world and put down roots. The divine motion toward the Father is not to be confused with human and superfluous bustle. The human exchange with its crossings should disturb the steady flow of the divine movement as little as possible. Every newcomer should take his place as quietly and smoothly as possible in the chain of the workers to take up the work where the last one left it.

This teaching of the Lord about the harvest and the great movement of the world toward the Father is not given without reason at the close of his meeting with the Samaritan woman. Had she not been there, the whole would have been merely a moral example. But as it is, one becomes aware that God's work is done very differently from human work. It is not good people who are relied upon, but believers. It is not the advanced and expert who are considered as workers in the sowing and reaping, but often enough the most impossible ones, humanly speaking. Neither is the work itself carried out according to human expectations. Men are always looking for a clear plan, like that of a farmer who sows his field. But God's plan is not transparent to view; the only thing one knows is that this plan will ultimately lead to God; one knows that it is God who calls, leads, and reaps. The ambiguity is part of his plan: he prepares people for eternal life by proving to them how differently God sows and reaps than they would. In a moment, he can turn a sinner who seemingly lived quite outside of grace into a disciple and instrument for the conversion of the Samaritans. Her destiny marks also the beginning of the overstretching of the

Christian, because God in his hidden plan seldom proceeds step by step but most often precipitately. Organic growth corresponds to our way of being and thinking, and we should indeed use our reason according to its laws in doing God's work. But no human reason is competent to interfere when God has spoken and developed his plan, however abrupt and anomalous it may appear to us. For ultimately, it is his work, his sowing, and his harvesting, and all our work is done in his name.

4:39–40. *Many Samaritans from that city believed in him because of the woman's testimony, "He told me all that I ever did." So when the Samaritans came to him, they asked him to stay with them; and he stayed there two days.*

It is sufficient for the Samaritans that the woman has told her story. She is known as a sinner, not a liar. Her compatriots who know her do not impute more sins to her than she actually has; they are not closed to what has always been good in her: her willing helpfulness, her readiness to love. So they respond to the message with which the woman so convincingly confronts them. They are prepared to allow themselves to be persuaded but demand further proofs. They need these proofs because their sense of justice, which is shown in their fair judgment about the woman, is not yet prompted by love. They go to the Lord and ask him to stay with them. The Lord welcomes any field of apostolate. He never converts a person for his own sake alone; in every conversion he sees the source of a new movement. Every conversion is a new beginning of growth in the Church, for none of them stops with the individual. The Lord accepts the invitation without reservation; he does so because they ask him—but also because he is touched to see that the woman so recently converted has begun to pass on what she has received.

4:41. *And many more believed because of his word.*

The first word was that of a sinful woman, but now the Word of God himself is heard. It is the same again as when the Lord began to baptize and immediately drew more crowds than John. As soon as the Lord comes on the scene, greater things take place.

The Church should in everything she does, therefore, rely much more on the Lord, on the immediate Word of God. She should not merely point a way to the Lord, but should come from God and speak from there. There is room for intermediate stages, symbols, examples; our neighbor has been given to us to help us. But all the help we can give toward conversion and deepening of religion comes to life only through this immediate coming from God. As the saints (3:14–15) have the task of mediating the immediate, so also all commentaries, spiritual books, and explanations have as their sole aim to mediate the immediacy of Sacred Scripture. No human word must be allowed to weaken or replace the original power of the word of God in the Church. All real power radiates from this word. Many a preacher loves preaching because he loves hearing himself speak. The word may perhaps have made an impact on him before, but now his own experience has become more important to him than the word itself; he talks about the effect the word produced in him and so of the effect God has through him—and, without noticing it, he talks only of himself.

4:42. *They said to the woman, "It is no longer because of your words that we believe, for we have heard for ourselves, and we know that this is indeed the Savior of the world."*

In saying this, they are not fully just. Something of the woman's witness remains part of their faith. Without the woman, they would not yet have found it. Shortly before, they were just to her—but outside of love. Now they become unjust. Human judgment moves to and fro like a pendulum if it is not anchored in the center of love. Though it is true that faith has to reach the Lord directly, the woman was the means, the interconnecting member that the Lord made use of. Here, too, of course, it was the Lord at work who converted the woman. But she prepared the soil and made it possible for them to accept the immediate message, and the Lord builds on this foundation.

The immediate conversion of the woman through the Lord means for her that she has been taken into his penetrating vision; it is contemplation. What the woman does in proclaiming the Lord she saw is action. From her contemplation flows action, and from her action, the contemplation in faith of the others. So far the relationship between contemplation and action was seen as unilateral: action flowing from contemplation. Here we see the complementary movement: contemplation as the fruit of action.

It is no longer because of your words that we believe. These words with which the Samaritans accost the woman contain a reproach that will quite often reappear later in the Church, whenever contemplation is overvalued at the expense of action. Contemplation can, of course, have the power of converting an individual or a crowd. But here its power is overestimated in its relationship to the power of action. Action is not played down because it is that of a woman and a sinner or because the Lord has made such an overwhelming impact on these people so as to take them wholly up into contemplation. The reason is a secret pride: they would like to owe their faith to the Lord alone. This secret pride, which is often present in contemplatives almost unconsciously, as a tendency will show itself repeatedly again later in the Church.

We have heard for ourselves. This, too, reveals a slight sense of superiority. To begin with, they naïvely believed because of the woman's testimony. Now they boast of their intimacy with the Lord. Already these first converts show themselves as all too human, and those who follow later will seldom be found free from this failing.

Their last words almost redeem these deficiencies. *We know that this is indeed the Savior of the world.* They know it because he said it but also because they belong to those who are saved. They are aware that the movement beginning with the woman has extended to them and is able to embrace the whole world. They believe because they have already a proof of the power of faith: it is gathering strength like a snowball and will spread in its movement to the ends of the world. What we have seen and experienced with our own eyes leads us to faith more quickly than what we have merely heard. These people saw the movement of faith arise and believe that it will spread without limit.

4:43. *After the two days he departed to Galilee.*

He does not allow them to contemplate him for longer than two days; he puts an early stop to it. Having once seen him does not entitle us to keep on seeing him. Above all, anyone who has once seen him should judge justly from now on. But their remarks to the woman show already that something is slightly out of focus. They are already taking pride in their immediacy to the Lord. Had he remained longer, they would have considered themselves his "intimates". Dealing familiarly with his humanity, they would have forgotten his divine word; their faith would have withered away without their noticing it. All false mysticism originates here, and all the aberrations that can occur in a mysticism that was at first genuine. They would have come to see themselves more and more as the

THE SAMARITAN WOMAN 153

"only true Christians" because they were contemplatives. The Lord himself gives the reason for his departure.

4:44. *For Jesus himself testified that a prophet has no honor in his own country.*

They are about to lower him by esteeming themselves his equals. They are about to turn their relationship with him into a "religion". They insert him into their personal, tribal, and civic structures and customs. They argue about him and make him the object of their gossip and surmising. Were he to stay longer, they would soon not hesitate to take over from him and claim the credit for themselves. This is always the case when a prophet comes into his own country. He may pass through it as the elemental fact that he is. Because he has to be this, he may not stay, for what is elemental cannot be organized in everyday terms.

4:45. *So when he came to Galilee, the Galileans welcomed him, having seen all that he had done in Jerusalem at the feast, for they too had gone to the feast.*

The Galileans believe because they already have seen something: the miracle in Jerusalem. They possess a certain favorable disposition toward him, which, however, is hardly more than the absence of rejection. They have no objection to his being the Messiah. But their belief is not urgent: it is satisfied and dull: they present the image of a mediocre community.

THE ROYAL OFFICIAL

4:46a. *So he came again to Cana in Galilee, where he had made the water wine.*

It happens repeatedly in the Christian life that the Lord lays a foundation to which he later returns. Here he returns to the place where he worked his first miracle. He comes as somebody different, but he returns. And in his return, he manifests himself as the same one he was. Last time it was the beginning, and much has changed in the meantime; people have changed through him, but he is who he is: the Son of the Father. So also in the Christian life there is not only the attempt to go forward on a way that unfolds like a spiral but also the grace that remains as the origin and must not be forgotten as it is the foundation. Once the Lord has intervened in a human life, has been close to and revealed himself to the person, other moments may come that seem to bear no exterior resemblance to this revelation; but the Lord returns, and the person must and may remember the moment of the origin. Progress does not mean seeing the Lord from ever-different angles. His own progress as the Father's Son consists, not of doing his unique work only once and then leaving it behind, but of being and remaining in every change the one Son of the Father.

4:46b–47. *And at Capernaum there was an official whose son was ill. When he heard that Jesus had come from Judea to Galilee, he went and begged him to come down and heal his son, for he was at the point of death.*

The father begs because he has heard that Jesus can do more than others, but he does not really believe. He comes to the Lord as to one who is said to have mysterious possibilities. He cannot believe that Christ is the Son of the Father or that miracles are possible today. But he does not want to leave anything undone. It cannot do any harm. He goes to the Lord with resignation, which is the opposite of faith. It is a resignation, not so much with regard to his son's death, which seems so close, but as a character trait of his heart. He sees in the Lord's miracles something like an accumulation of accidental happenings; but still, he hopes that he will not prove the exception when he knocks at the Lord's door. However, he is not closed to faith; he has an attitude of nonopposition, even a certain inclination toward belief. But he does not fully believe in miracles and makes his belief dependent on the fate of his son. He would not be able to continue to believe if he had to accept the death of his son. He resembles those of weak faith—though he himself has no faith at all as yet—a person of little faith that will evaporate when shaken. But he also resembles those unbelievers who are not hostile to faith and want to show their goodwill, which they desire to be understood as a first step. Their goodwill is not Christian faith but a sort of moral faith. This official is a respectable person who lives according to strict principles and loves his son—even if for himself—and he is prepared to love the Lord in the same way—for himself—in gratitude for a service rendered. He carefully reflects on everything. He knows exactly where he stands. This gives him a certain sympathy for the faith of others; he respects its role as a possible support for their weakness. At any rate, he does not reject it out of hand.

4:48–49. Jesus therefore said to him, "Unless you see signs and wonders you will not believe." The official said to him, "Sir, come down before my child dies."

People first want a proof of his power; then they are ready to obey. Their faith resembles a business transaction, a contract. The man does not understand that faith in Christ becomes a mutual surrender. He sees first of all the mutual advantage. He sees his readiness to believe as a kind of pledge for future dependence, for sacrifices that he will have to make. For he is already calculating what the Lord will take from him and demand from him. He is aware that the Lord will not ask for money; but even faith appears to him like the settling of a bill. He would almost rather lay an enormous sum on the table and be rid of all obligation, for the spiritual demand appears much harder to him than any other could be. Such a transaction seems to him not noble enough as far as the Lord is concerned; he still has no idea that one can give and at the same time be the one immeasurably receiving. This experience is wholly lacking to him; he has never had it before in his life. And he judges everything according to his own experience. He has never met real love and real happiness, for the dynamic of love consists in giving and being given. He finds it embarrassing that the Lord first of all demands the reversal in him of the relationship between seeing and believing, receiving and giving. He moves on to the practical issue: *"Sir, come down before my child dies."* His son, not the Lord, is important to him. The Lord is only an instrument. He presses on; he did not come to hold long conversations. He is looking for the deed, nothing else.

4:50–54. Jesus said to him, "Go; your son will live." The man believed the word that Jesus spoke to him and went his way. As he was going down, his servants met him and told him that his son was living. So he asked them the hour when he began to mend, and they said to him, "Yesterday at the seventh hour the fever left him." The father knew that was the hour when Jesus had said to him, "Your son will live"; and he himself believed, and all his household. This was now the second sign that Jesus did when he had come from Judea to Galilee.

The Lord's words *your son will live* signal two transitions: from sickness to health and from unbelief to faith. The Lord never worked a miracle that was purely physical. All his miracles are directed to faith and bring it into being. He works miracles only according to the Father's will, to prepare the way for him. Each of his signs is given within his mission in order to open access to the Father. And that is why all his signs have something additional in common: each of them, even the smallest, is a sacrifice the Lord offers. If men would believe as they should, without signs and wonders, the Lord's way and mission would be easier. Each sign he gives is an additional burden for him and increases his future suffering. Each miracle costs him pain, because he has to break through the opposition of unbelief through suffering.

The man believes and goes. He, too, has been changed. He has not yet seen the miracle, but he believes. Part of the miracle took place in him. On the way he meets the servants, still unbelievers, who mediate to him the proof and the vision. They announce the physical cure of his son, but already in the Lord's presence he has understood that the life of his son above all is the life of faith, and he knows this has been given him as well.

The hour is right; he believes with all his household. He first believed before receiving the proof, and now the proof overwhelms him. In contrast to his son, he is not consciously aware at what moment his Christian conversion began; he becomes aware of it only afterward.

The son, however, knows the hour when his faith was born: it coincides with his cure. Simply and gratefully he believes. From the sickness of unbelief, he awakens to faith; he becomes whole in this faith. He understands his cure immediately as a spiritual transformation. The servants believe out of devotedness. They believe because their masters do. The faith of father and son is immediate and direct; that of the servants, mediated through their masters. This is the image of a Christian household and its graduated and combined unity of faith.

THE SICK MAN AT BETHESDA

5:1–4. *After this there was a feast of the Jews, and Jesus went up to Jerusalem. Now there is in Jerusalem by the Sheep Gate a pool, in Hebrew called Bethzatha, which has five porticoes. In these lay a multitude of invalids, blind, lame, paralyzed [waiting for the moving of the water; for an angel of the Lord went down at certain seasons into the pool, and troubled the water; whoever stepped in first after the troubling of the water was healed of whatever disease he had].*

Perhaps there is a meaning in the name of the pool by the Sheep Gate. Here we hear for the first time of sheep, a motif that will become so important later on in Saint John. People are gathered together here who in their simplicity give the impression of a herd of sheep. Sheep move us by their simplicity and vulnerability, and the Lord passing through this place is already moved and touched by such simplicity. He sees in them the image of those who are guiltless. But they have all been caught up in a complicated system, a spiritual thorn hedge from which they cannot free themselves. This makes them images of a great part of humanity. They hate their infirmities and do not look at these as a blessing. But since they are caught up in them and have to live with them, they have invented a story, a myth, a mixture of religion and medicine that enables them to live and gives a meaning and justification to their illnesses. The whole is superstition, and the cures that take place are illusionary miraculous healings. There are different groups among the sick. Not all are really ill; some of them have somehow slithered into the state of being sick and do not find the way and strength to leave illness behind. Exteriorly they continue to play the role of being sick because it appears to them in some way interesting and advantageous. Or perhaps they have lost the courage to be well, though they are very conscious that they have no longer any reason for holding onto their sickness. All of them need an exterior occasion to get well, a theory of healing, in order to find an excuse for or dramatize their transition back into normal life. It is too little for them simply to be well again; they need a sensational cure. Only if their cure attracts more attention to them than their illness are they prepared to leave the latter behind.

They are an image of those who are aware of their interior sickness without being able to rid themselves of it and to want to do so: sick in faith and morals. Deep within, they know that there is only one salvation, the Lord. But him they do not want; they turn to one of the thousands of philosophies, "churches", sects, myths, and superstitions; they are inventing ever-new systems that are nothing more than ever-new substitutes for faith to which they cannot rise. Like a conglomeration of huts built around the Church, these short-lived attempts are substitutes for the single truth, which demands nothing more than the courage of complete surrender. This courage, which would mean health for these people at the Sheep Gate, is what is lacking to them. And through this crowd the Lord now passes and performs a miracle as a sign among them.

This new miracle has a certain resemblance to the previous one. For the royal official and the individuals by the Sheep Gate have a great fear that the Lord may deprive them of something. Both excuse themselves from believing by pointing to their goodwill. What these sick people cherish is a substitute, and as such it brings them "comfort". They have resigned themselves to their system, their sect: Why turn the whole world into Christians and Catholics? But this resignation has become part of their ideology; consciously they have entered a byway, so that the great and central call of the Lord may pass them by. These people all wear blinkers and distorting spectacles. They are unable to see the Lord as he is because they are not on his direct path. So the Lord is forced to come himself into their hospital and fetch them back. The official was able to ask the Lord himself. These here cannot do this for themselves, for they have decided that what they "believe" is sufficient for them. A nonbeliever can have a flash of insight and begin to believe. But one who has created for himself a substitute for belief in the Lord and relies on it can no longer see the Lord; the Lord himself has to come and smash his cardboard construction. His appearance alone, however, is not enough, for the sick man is so entrenched in his system that a mere appearance would not impress him. He would receive the Lord and his appearance into his system and give him a place in it. Therefore, the Lord can here come only as destroyer of the system. He must show himself as one who has power over the system, as miracle worker. He could draw the attention of these invalids by the pool in no other way.

5:5–7. One man was there, who had been ill for thirty-eight years. When Jesus saw him and knew that he had been lying there a long time, he said to him, "Do you want to be healed?" The sick man answered him, "Sir, I have no man to put me into the pool when the water is troubled, and while I am going another steps down before me."

The man Jesus meets really is a sick person, and he has been ill for longer than the whole span of the Lord's earthly life. The beginning of his illness reaches back to a different level from the present one: it reaches back into the Old Covenant. Moreover, the sick man believes that he can be healed. But he does not see a practical possibility. It is this man the Lord addresses. He does not heal someone who is not really ill or anyone who firmly counts on being healed by natural means. He chooses a genuinely sick man who has not yet despaired of the "system" but recognizes that it does not fit his own case. He believes the cause to be a good one—that is his luck, for he is naïve, open to faith—but he does not see it as meant for him, in which he is also lucky, for he has not yet made his personal cure dependent on the system. He is looking for another kind of truth, which could become of practical consequence for him.

The Lord takes no notice of the system. He could have carried the sick man into the water and become the "man" who is missing to him. But the Lord heals him completely outside of the system. He heals him by his word. He not only heals him but expressly frees him from the system. Had the Lord entered into the system, had he carried the sick man in a sort of anonymous love into the water without betraying anything of his mission, he would not have acted as the Son of God, as the Lord. He would have supported the system, while, on the contrary, he has come to abolish all closed systems that men have invented as bars against the openness of faith and love. He would have remained in his contemplation without acting as the Son. The man who was cured would have continued to believe that the bearer was merely a helper and that the cure was due to the system.

5:8. *Jesus said to him, "Rise, take up your pallet, and walk."*

Take up your pallet on which you have lain all these years; destroy the system to which you have so long been fettered. No memory must be retained of it. No looking back on the sickness. The sick man must not leave any roots in the place; even the pallet must be taken away, so that the new faith has no more links, no relation to the substitute. The Lord demands the whole: his mission, coming from the Father, is the only root from which he lives, from which his faithful also have to live, and this mission has nothing in common with any cosmic powers and magic angels in the twilight of human sensationalism.

5:9. *And at once the man was healed, and he took up his pallet and walked. Now that day was the Sabbath.*

The Lord grants healing to the sick man in the form of a command: "*Take up your pallet and walk.*" And the sick man becomes whole in the form of obedience. And if physical health means at the same time health of the soul through faith, as it did in the previous case, then the sick man received faith through his obedience. The way from obedience to faith becomes also the way of grace to faith. Grace would then mean for man the possibility of obeying. The Lord announces by the same word the gift of grace and the demand of following. In giving, he calls. But this demand, wherever it is made, is not of the nature that the royal official and these people here feared, for it is an innermost part of the gift of the Lord. It belongs to it so closely that we meet it wherever the Lord gives: in prayer, in meditation, in each individual sacrament.

The sick man will come to faith: we are not told whether this happens on account of the gift of the healing or on account of his obedience to grace. Believing after a grace received is not difficult, for faith is often very close to gratitude; this is easy. The way from obedience to faith, however, can appear difficult to some. In this man, both meet: the easy and the difficult aspects of faith. He receives a miracle, but this miracle immediately contains a demand: to make a clean break and leave a situation behind that has lasted almost forty years. For such a step to be possible, an attitude is necessary that is the prerequisite of true obedience: humility. Even in sin, we may not be closed up and congested by sin. The naked demand that the Lord makes in the name of the Father without linking it to a promise requires a naked humility that makes obedience and faith possible. For nothing resembles love (from which all faith is born) more than humility. The whole is a work of grace as a way into grace: as humbly obedient a man walks within the grace offered, and as a believer as soon as grace is accepted. This is now happening on a Sabbath.

5:10. *So the Jews said to the man who was cured, "It is the sabbath, it is not lawful for you to carry your pallet."*

The Jews see only that their regulation has been broken and the man is doing what is forbidden by the law. Their law knows no exception, so they completely ignore the fact of the cure, which is obvious to all. Judaism and Christianity clash even before there is a conscious confrontation and elucidation of viewpoints. What the Lord does is already condemned by the Jews before they have examined the cause. In this, they are the image of those who in their pettiness and narrowness are constantly scandalized because they do not see the large horizon; they stumble forever at the periphery of great things because, instead of keeping their eyes on these, they look only at their own feet—which prevents them from walking. Their field of vision is blocked by their own narrowness, which provides at once the next stone to stumble over. Everywhere they see only details that do not leave them either time or strength for the main object. Their law is nearer and closer to them than God. The vessel is more important to them than the content. This ritualism continues in the

New Covenant—how should it not? It is present wherever ceremony becomes more important than the Lord and his presence in the Church, the rule and paragraph more meaningful than what is regulated by it, the rubric of an ecclesial act more important than this act itself.

5:11. *But he answered them, "The man who healed me said to me, 'Take up your pallet, and walk.'"*

The man who is questioned is still ignorant of the identity of his healer. He has only the faith of love, not the faith of recognition. He has the faith that is born solely from love and can be guided anywhere this may lead. He feels that this faith will lead to more and demand more, that he has received only a seed; he knows it in an unreflected way, in sheer gratitude of heart. He has received and is prepared for a return; he has already begun. He loves the one who has healed him, and his gratitude prompts him to do what he said to him. Such a faith from gratitude is deeply embedded in human nature; but if the giver is human, he has to take great care not to abuse this faith. He will have to pass it on to God straightaway. The Lord does not need this caution because he himself is God, and as the Son he passes everything on to the Father. In his purity, however, he shows us the danger that lies in tying men to oneself when one is still oneself tied to sin. Sin is precisely that which does not lead to God but, itself tied, ties others also.

5:12. *They asked him, "Who is the man who said to you, 'Take up your pallet, and walk'?"*

They keep on asking from curiosity. It matters little to them whether they know the answer already or not. They ask from malice. They see that this man carries his bed on a Sabbath without evil intent. They try to drive a wedge into his simplicity; they seek to create confusion and complication. They are asking, not because they want to know themselves, but to arouse doubts and questions in the man who has been healed. Their aim is to distract him from his open intent, to disperse and, if possible, destroy the simple wholeness of faith that he has become, to introduce something destructive into his soul, to pass on their malicious agitation under the pretext of knowledge and research. Their sole intention is to sow the problematic by which they themselves live into the souls of others whose wholeness irritates them and whose calm makes them still more restless.

5:13. *Now the man who had been healed did not know who it was, for Jesus had withdrawn, as there was a crowd in the place.*

The man who was healed did not ask the Lord who he was. His need for understanding was fully satisfied in a believing love. In spite of his age and his long illness, he received in his cure a childlike faith; his problems were solved by the Lord's intervention in his life; everything has been put in order within him. He has somehow arrived; he has found the calm that faith always brings, though he is hardly conscious of it. It is a simple participation in the Lord, the happiness of one converted who turns to the Lord like the flower to the sun simply because he feels that love is here, and everything else remains open and in the Lord's hand.

5:14. *Afterward, Jesus found him in the temple, and said to him, "See, you are well! Sin no more, that nothing worse befall you."*

That is the only word with which the Lord sends him on his way: "*Sin no more!*" He does not explain his past sin to him, for he sees his soul open before him. He covers up all that is past without looking at it or going through it in detail. He only shows him the danger that remains: that of sinning again. He does not tie him to himself but lets him go freely, for he is sure of his love. This bond is already in order. The man knows that sin is incompatible with this bond of love to the Lord. He understands that sin would separate him from the Lord, and so he is aware that the other is the Lord, his Lord. And, at the same time, also that separation from this Lord through sin would be the only evil that can still befall him. This warning from the Lord implies that anyone who has received special personal graces from him is even more in danger of falling away, even more ready to do so. For he is more closely bound by this grace than others are. However small the sin that he commits appears, it is more capable of coming between him and the Lord than that of a man who did not receive such a special grace. A speck of dust can be sufficient to stop the delicate work. Everything is built on personal fidelity and no longer on the keeping of the Commandments and a moral code.

5:15. *The man went away and told the Jews that it was Jesus who had healed him.*

He does it partly because he has been questioned; but even more because he now knows in whom he believes, and this knowledge united with his faith impels him to proclaim it. The question of the Jews obliges him to reply to them in particular; the knowledge about the Lord adds the further obligation not only to answer those who ask but also to proclaim to all he can reach what he knows and believes. He is aware that he has to imitate in his small human measure the immeasurable self-giving of the Lord. He understands that his knowledge was given him to be passed on, that the miracle worked for him was not for himself alone but also for others, for all who can be reached by it. In his conversation with the Lord, he experienced contemplation; now it flows over into action. He is conscious of this, but his primary faith itself leads him to this.

5:16. *And this was why the Jews persecuted Jesus, because he did this on the sabbath.*

They take the law for a greater obligation than love, so they cannot but be scandalized. In their law, there is no space for the space that embraces the law itself. Their law is rigid, but love can be moved and stretched. They are all the more comfortable with the rigid as they themselves are wobbly, unsure, and full of problems. The law is their security against themselves.

THE CONFERRING OF JUDGMENT

5:17. *But Jesus answered them, "My Father is working still, and I am working."*

The Sabbath law on which the Jews are hardening is the Father's law. And the Father works on this law even today. But the Son also is at work, and thus the Old Law becomes widened out. Until now the Father alone was at work, for the Son was hidden in the Father. Now the Son comes forward, and the Father works together with him, in him, and through him. The Son's law, which is the law of love, explodes the letter of the Old Law, which has become reduced to the letter because men have not accepted it as something alive but allowed it to become rigid. The Son, however, is the Living One who must be understood and accepted as such through the letter.

So far mankind has had relations with the Father. Now Father and Son are working together, and the Son's work contains that of the Father. Thus, the law is widened out, because the work of God has become enlarged. True, in the Old Law also, the Son was included in the Father's work; already the Covenant of justice contained love as seed within itself. But now that the Son has taken on himself the sacrifice of being separate from the Father, his work becomes more personal and can be recognized as that of the Son distinct from the Father's. And after the return of the Son, the work of the Father, the Son, and the Holy Spirit will be united again in one single activity. But this unity after differentiation will be much richer for the world than that of the beginning, for the love revealed in the separation and suffering of the Incarnation was not in vain. The Trinity is much more fruitful during the earthly life of Christ than it was before the Incarnation; it will be most fruitful from the Ascension of Christ to eternal life. The personal work of the Son as Son remains for all eternity, even though included in the Trinity, marked by his redeeming Incarnation. It is as if through it the whole Trinity had become more distinguishable and accessible to us. The Son's work was so dynamic that his divine life can become dynamic in us; he has thrown light on the trinitarian relations in such a way that we feel addressed by them in our innermost being; in his Person he has established a personal relationship between the Trinity and each man. This is his work, which is enduring at the same time as it is in constant progress.

5:18. *This was why the Jews sought all the more to kill him, because he not only broke the sabbath but also called God his Father, making himself equal with God.*

He makes their God his own God: that is what embitters the Jews. Calmly he develops the eternal relationship of the Son to his Father. Through this he opposes their secret absolute agitation and remains unimpressed by their adhesion to the law. No discussion (by which they, after all, live) is possible with him. And since they cannot get at him by any approach, they see the necessity of doing away with him; they know no means other than death. That the Son's work could reach beyond death is unthinkable for them. The Lord's end means for them the end of all the relationships he reveals to them. After that God will again be their God as they know him.

THE CONFERRING OF JUDGMENT 171

5:19. *Jesus said to them, "Truly, truly, I say to you, the Son can do nothing of his own accord, but only what he sees the Father doing; for whatever he does, that the Son does likewise."*

Everything the Son has he has from the Father; he can therefore do nothing without him. But the Father has given everything to the Son; he cannot do anything without the Son. So they are equal in what they do. The Jews look for deeds; it is deeds that count for them. They know the Father's deeds from Scripture, and the Son's deeds are worked before their eyes. They are not open for anything other than deeds, and on this very point they can examine and recognize the equality of Father and Son. But the fact that the Lord puts the stress on this enrages them still further. The deed to which this particular verse refers is not identical with the work mentioned before. The work comprises a whole area of action, a period, a development taking place. The deed means a single act complete in itself. In doing something, Father and Son act as one, but in their work they distinguish themselves from each other while acting in unison. It could appear that there is a contradiction between the differentiation in working stressed before (verse 17) and the unity in action stressed afterward (verses 19–21). But it is the second statement that explains the first. And it also has to be remembered that here only the beginning, the origin of the New Covenant from the Old, is made visible. The first statement contains the entire principle of the New Covenant; the ones that follow show this New Covenant only in its first beginning. Only those who know already can appreciate that the branch of the Son leaves the stem of the Father and begins to work independently. Only on the Cross, in the godforsakenness of the Son with regard to the Father, will this meaning become fully comprehensible. And only as seen from the Cross do the final statements of this speech, which again recall the full principle of the New Covenant (verse 22), become fully clear: where the Father out of love separates himself from the Son in love.

The Lord can explain the meaning of his own actions only by beginning with his unity with the Father. His whole personal being comes from the Father and is wholly rooted in him. So he cannot do anything without the Father. He expresses his working together with the Father by stressing first of all the unity of the action. Only then can the differentiation be shown as a fuller explanation of the unity.

5:20. *For the Father loves the Son, and shows him all that he himself is doing; and greater works than these will he show him, that you may marvel.*

Here the Lord speaks for the first time of the love between Father and Son. And at once in the beautiful sense that the Father in his love for the Son can have no secret before him; he *"shows him all that he himself is doing"*. And in the still higher sense that out of love he not only shows him all he is doing but allows him to work together with him. These works are not complete but are open to the greater things that the Father will do and will let the Son do. What has been done so far has merely been introduction and indication of ever-higher movement. As yet the Jews have seen little: healing of sick people, perhaps the conversion of the Samaritan woman. The greater things they will marvel at are still in the future. For the Father wants them to marvel. He wants it because he is concerned for them, because he loves them. What the greater things will be the Lord does not reveal at present. His future path remains still hidden. He only points out that love is the meaning of this widening path: the Father loves me, and in me he loves you

THE CONFERRING OF JUDGMENT 173

also. He indicates the direction this increase will take in the following words.

5:21. *For as the Father raises the dead and gives them life, so also the Son gives life to whom he will.*

In his love for the Son and to give the Son the joy of being loved by men (and of seeing the Father loved also), the Father is ready to do ever-greater works. For those already living and loving, small miracles are sufficient; for those hardened, more striking miracles are necessary, such as even transcend the barriers of life and death: the raising of the dead. But the Lord never works a physical miracle without it being also a spiritual one. Neither does he ever use a man merely as a means in order to work a miracle for the benefit of others. Raising someone from the dead on his lips, therefore, also means awakening him to faith and, therefore, to love. The Lord has not yet died on the Cross, and so death still remains and the kingdom of death, the underworld. A person raised to life is for the present called back to this earthly life in order to live, believe, and love here below. But even such a raising from the dead already means the shattering of the boundary between life and death. One can see already: the circles of life will become larger; life here on earth, where we love today, will gradually include death itself, and the kingdom of Hades will, through the supreme miracle of raising from the dead, become incorporated into the Son's Kingdom of love.

In this life, of course, the raising from bodily death and that from spiritual death do not always go together; the first is rather a parable of the second. The two miraculous cures only point to the supernatural vocation to faith and to the following of Christ, which the apostles received and to which the Lord invites all whom he encounters and who are not closed to the call. The choice is his: *he gives life to whom he will.* But it is in no way a chance occurrence. For he chooses all who are turned to him, all who are dissatisfied with themselves. It is his choice if they are turned to him. In his relationship with his chosen, a mutual commitment takes place: the Lord in his choice commits himself to granting faith, and the chosen one commits himself to accepting it. It is possible for one touched by Christ to resist faith. Then the consequences will be different for him than for others who do not know the Lord. For he is no longer a pagan; he is already joined to the chosen Christian people. Here, not to believe, not to love, means turning away from the Lord with full knowledge and free will. Nothing is said here about raising such a dead man to life.

5:22. *The Father judges no one, but has given all judgment to the Son.*

Here the New Testament comes to its fullness: the Son himself is fully at work. The beginning was shown in verse 17. For the Father sent the Son into his separate existence out of love, and in love, and has given him his own love to accompany him into his mission and to enable him to achieve what has always been the Son's characteristic and desire: love for his brothers. The Father's renunciation of the Son is born from love for the sake of love. And to authenticate exteriorly this renunciation as a work of love, the Father gives all judgment, which is his own innermost characteristic, into the Son's hand, so that henceforth there will be no judgment of justice but only a judgment of love. Because a New Covenant is going to be established in the Son, the Father has to give the judgment of love to the Son, and all threats of the Old Testament, all the terrors and prophecies of justice, are being dissolved in love. All who have lived under the Old Covenant and come from there, those standing between the two Covenants, have to make a decision and recognize that something new has happened. To make this decision possible for them and to demonstrate that the old is really fulfilled in the new, the Son must be invested with the Father's power of judgment and authorized by it. The new must not come in any way other than as fulfillment of the old. But neither can it be achieved by anything less than a new birth, so that the old is demolished rather than fulfilled. The hard closed circle of justice must give way to the limitless expansion of love. What until now has been done in the name of God will in the future be done in the name of the Father and the Son and the Holy Spirit.

5:23a. *That all may honor the Son, even as they honor the Father.*

Until now, all honored the Son hidden in the Father by honoring the Father. Now the Son is made visible, and he must be honored exteriorly and separately by himself, for the Father has invested the Son with power as distinct from himself. But this conferring of authority does not abolish his Sonship, and the New Covenant does not abolish the Old. The judgment of justice was not a mistake and cannot be replaced by another; it remains in existence in the law of love, which could unfold only from the foundation of justice. The transition from the first to the second lies in the fact that the Father, who judges, sees in the Son the perfect just man, for the Son is the sinless and guiltless one, coming forth from the Father's justice and fulfilling it perfectly. When the Father in judgment looks at the Son with the eyes of justice, he sees nothing that would call for judgment; since everything is right and just in him, there is nothing to be judged. Justice therefore has nothing to look for, and judgment naturally dissolves into love, which is the greater reality, born from the fulfillment of judgment. Where nothing remains to be measured and judged, there is room for the immeasurable, for love. In the same way, the Son's readiness to be judged by the Father also dissolves into the same love.

Since the Father has given all judgment to the Son, and the judgment has already become one of love between Father and Son, the Son also cannot pass judgment, which is already dissolved, on men, except as the judgment of love he himself has experienced and received from the Father. Verse 19 here receives its deeper meaning: the Son does only what he sees the Father doing (to him). Verse 17 is also explained anew: though the Son does nothing but what he sees the Father doing, he brings about something completely different from what existed before: he replaces the Father's judgment of justice with the judgment of love. This takes place because the Son comes forth from the Father and takes his place on the side of man: and so he draws the inner divine judgment between Father and Son across to the world, so that the Father can no longer make a distinction between a judgment of justice and a judgment of love. For the Son has become one of us without distinction between himself and other men. In this way, the Father's judgment has been taken out of his hands and has passed as a judgment of love to the Son, who accepts it from the Father as he has experienced it in himself. The Son has never experienced anything but love from the Father, not even in judgment; and so he can never pass any judgment on men other than that of love. The Father loved the Son especially in judgment, and so the Son will love his neighbor, all men, especially in judgment. Only one judgment the Father cannot pass on: his eternal judgment of love over the Son. It is into this judgment that the Son wants to introduce those who are his, so that all can stand before the Father as he himself does. The whole of the Son's office of judgment has no purpose other than to bring about this last judgment of the Father. All that brings men to this moment where as aspirants to paradise they are presented to the Father by the Son, all that serves their purification and training toward standing in the same place as the Son before the Father, all this is every time an act of the loving judgment of the Son. Purgatory, for example, which we see as an act of justice, is seen in this light as nothing but an act of love of the Son, who wants to purify us so that this substitution that makes us sons of the Father can come about.

This substitution explains the way in which the Son deals with men in his encounters, how he makes use of those whom he chooses to raise to life (verse 21). All whom he converts he converts to his love and allows them to work from then on in his love and for him. Because they do his work, because they work in his name, they are judged just because of this decision of working for his love. To be just does not mean here without sin; it means working within the Lord's love. What is meant is not primarily the relationship of office, of priesthood and succession, but the immediate relationship of love, which all possess who live in the grace of the Lord in the service of his love. Because their intention corresponds to that of the Lord, because the Lord's love radiates from them and is passed on through them, their whole work is considered just, and the worker's sinfulness is forgotten. Of course, the work must really flow from the spirit of the Lord's love. In no way can the consciousness of being thus included in the Lord's justice serve as an excuse to anyone for evil deeds, and no one can claim "good works" as substituting for sins. But the saying about the end justifying the means has here the good meaning that God will excuse the foolish and useless means and will look at them kindly and make use of them if people are trying to bring about his ends. These works are sanctified in the measure in which they are done in love.

Those who in the Old Covenant stood under the Father's judgment honored him. For men normally do not love and serve without expecting some return. The Father's judgment was a constant warning to them that kept them reverent. They divined something of the Father's greatness in it; they were educated by it to the sense of his divinity. In the law of Moses and its threats, the transcendence of God was ever placed before their eyes. This respect could sometimes spur them on to keep God's law. And to ensure the same respect that is due to God now also to the Son in the world, God entrusted in the Incarnation the whole of judgment to him. The Son, however, who lives out of love, in love transforms this respect offered him, which is due to his divinity, at once into a matter of love.

As the objective judgment of justice was changed into a judgment of love, so now also the subjective feeling of reverence is transformed into one of love. Love fulfills fear and brings it to its innermost truth, but, even more, it overcomes fear and makes it obsolete. So the circle that began with the previous verse is closed again. Once again it is only an apparent difference that is seen between Father and Son, insofar as the Father gives the justice of the Old Covenant to the Son, who as such is wholly love. In reality, the Son himself transforms this justice into love and gives it back transformed to the Father. And the conferring of justice from the Father to the Son is in itself an act of the Father's love. The Father is not stricter than the Son. His infinite love consists in leaving everything to the Son in love and so giving it out of his hand. And the Son's love is no other than the Father's love become visible, for it does nothing but what it sees the Father doing. There remain those who do not want to be judged by the Son's judgment of love, who voluntarily withdraw from this judgment. These have to be judged by the Father because they have rejected the love of the Son (in whom all the Father's love is invested).

5:23b. *He who does not honor the Son does not honor the Father who sent him.*

From the moment when the Son stands before the world in the Father's mission, it is impossible to overlook this mission and not to honor the Son, whom the Father has sent and authorized. As soon as the New Covenant appears, the Old Covenant loses its justification. The Son, of course, fulfills his mission in a personal way as the Son, but it remains the Father's mission. Once the Son has appeared, no one can look for another way to the Father except through the Son, for the whole of the Father's love is summed up in him, and he loves the world only in the Son. All who henceforth have to do with the Father or the Son have to deal with the Father *and* the Son. All must in some way participate in the dynamic movement of the Trinity. For the Father is he who has sent the Son eternally and in time, and access to him is only through the Son. The Son, however, is the living way to the Father; he fills the whole breadth of the way so that there is no space besides. He is the total grace of the Father, the only access to him.

5:24. *Truly, truly, I say to you, he who hears my word and believes him who sent me, has eternal life; he does not come into judgment, but has passed from death to life.*

For the Lord it is all one thing: to hear his word and believe in the one who sent him. He has shown clearly that he and the Father are one and that to believe in the Father can now only mean to believe the word of him whom he has sent. Christ cannot convert anyone to himself as Son without expressly leading him to faith in the Father. For a short time longer, the possibility will exist in the world of belief in God without hearing the word of Christ; the Jews who have not yet had to decide for Christ will have this opportunity. But there is no possibility of believing in Christ without believing in the Father; for anyone who has encountered Christ, this Jewish possibility is no longer open. For the grace that comes from Christ, the grace of his word, leads only to the trinitarian Father, to the Father of the Word, not to the Father of the Old Testament. In the New Testament, the Word and so also the Father of the Word can no longer be dispensed with. No one can separate the Son's teaching from the Person of the Son; for he *is* the Father's Word.

Anyone who hears the Father's Word and believes him *has eternal life*. It is sufficient to believe in order to be alive, in order to live eternally. For faith as the Son proclaims and expects it concerns not merely a part of man or his intellect only but everything in him, whole and entire. It is closely linked to love and contains hope. Such faith is the seed from which everything develops in the love of the Father and the Son. It is seed, initiation, beginning, revelation, opening, readiness. It is filled with the love of the Lord. His grace nurtures and waters it, so to say, so that it can flower into eternal life. It receives eternal life not merely as future reward; it contains it already, because faith together with the body of Christ is so alive that it cannot die. And this for all eternity, because the love of the Lord is eternally alive.

Whoever has this faith *does not come into judgment*, for he already now lives in love. He lives in the love constantly given him by the Lord and in the love he constantly returns to the Lord, because the Lord gave it to him. There is no room for judgment here. A judgment always means a standstill: the one to be judged is stopped on his way, taken hold of, examined, and weighed. The judgment interrupts life. But here no interruption is possible; the Lord himself could not stay the lover in his course, because he himself was the first to love him. He is like a bullet shot that cannot be recalled. In the Old Testament, judgment was a reality because of the obstacles and limitations posed by the law. In the New Testament, it is unknown because there are no obstacles that love could not surmount. Every barrier placed in its way becomes a new stimulation. There is now only the open road into what is ever greater, pure intensification, constant increase. He has *passed from death to life*. There is only one life, which is faith. Everything else is dead. Only faith is receptive for the life that is love. Without faith, one can give to one's neighbor what is called charity among men, but one gives it to oneself in the neighbor, not to the Lord. Outside of the Lord's love, we can only love our neighbor as ourselves; the measure of our giving corresponds to what we want others to do for us; man himself is the measure of his love. Showing compassion in helping one's neighbor is done with the thought of receiving the same compassion in a similar situation. This love of neighbor is then a kind of insurance policy for the neighbor's love for oneself. That is not the living love of the Lord. This begins with faith; here the transition takes place from death to life, from me to you, from self-centeredness to the life of love.

Faith is and remains alive only if in union with the Body of Christ in the *Eucharist*. He left us the Eucharist as a living proof of his love, because we who are trying to live by his love are ever in need of this proof. As faith is a tiny seed, a beginning, almost nothing, and yet everything comes forth from this smallest of seeds, so also the Eucharist is the smallest and most unobtrusive thing, a dry crumb of bread, but it produces fullness of life, as love is produced from faith. Faith and the Eucharist are one in this way: through faith the sinner is transformed, passing inexplicably through the Lord's word to the eternal life of a saint in heaven; through the word of the priest, the wafer, which is nothing in itself, is transformed into eternal life in such an ultimate way that this life does not come to an end when the Host is consumed but goes on living in those who consume it. The sinner passes away once for all in the act of faith, the substance of the bread in the word of transubstantiation. Both words are final.

Eucharist and faith form a unity also because the reception of the Eucharist strengthens faith as it imparts an increase in love—the small gesture of love in the recipient is amplified by the Lord's self-giving—and bestows a sharing in eternal life, for the Eucharist in its inmost being is eternal. It is eternal because the Lord's flesh is eternal and immortal, no matter at which moment of time and history the transubstantiation takes place; it is the eternal Spirit of the Lord who changes the temporal bread into his eternal flesh through the priest. Man's faith thus finds its fulfillment in the eternal Eucharist. But the Eucharist is no less fulfilled in man's faith. If no one were to believe, no one to hunger for the Eucharist, the Eucharist would cease to be. Only because people are hungry does bread exist in the world. The Eucharist and man's faith, however, do not exist on the same level; but though we live in total dependence on the Lord, he gives us a sign of his love by making himself also dependent on us.

Faith and Eucharist are therefore always a transition to eternal life. In the sinner, death lies at the beginning of the movement; eternal life is the goal. The Lord in the Eucharist cannot be said to pass from death to life each time again. The question of beginning is irrelevant here; only that of the goal counts. But still, there is each time a beginning, which leads to eternal life, and a Real Presence, and this is the presence of his love encompassed by our faith. This love is his beginning.

Finally, this mutual empowering of Father and Son is the birth of *thankfulness*. To give thanks lies on the level of justice, but where this level is transcended into love a new attitude emerges: thankfulness. It springs from God's being, from the relationship between Father and Son, and can therefore become a way and beginning of love when it is born among men. It is a wholly self-giving love. To give thanks is something owed for a service rendered; there is a measurable equity between a service done and the remuneration that is owed. But as soon as the one who has been served becomes aware that the service was rendered in love, that it was an expression of love, the proportionate thanks becomes open-ended thankfulness. Even when it is thankfulness for a service rendered, this limited act of service is overlooked in the sense that it is transcended. In the limited act, unlimited love is seen, and the recognition is felt that this love cannot be paid for by mere thanks. The center of thankfulness passes from the one who gives thanks to the one who receives it. If a man has saved another man's life, the man whose life was saved will thank him, but if he is a grateful person, he will see all his future life as owed to his savior; in everything he does, thinks, suffers, and achieves, there will be something of his benefactor to whom he owes his life. If his own being becomes so open that it appears to be entirely a function of his savior, room is made for God in the soul. What so far was a limited giving of thanks becomes true love, which does not seek to repay because it desires to remain in debt to the beloved. At that moment, the other truly becomes his neighbor. And the more this love of neighbor transcends the debt owed in order to become true love for the person himself, the more it begins to resemble the love between Father and Son, which needs no service because beyond all mutual gifts it is directed straight to the Person of the other, lavishing its inexhaustible treasures of love on the beloved in pure love without thinking of service and gratitude owed.

5:25. *Truly, truly, I say to you, the hour is coming, and now is, when the dead will hear the voice of the Son of God, and those who hear will live.*

The hour is coming and now is. From the moment the Lord appears in the world, everything that is coming already is. It is in him. For the Host, the hour is coming but is here already. The Consecration comes, but he who comes is already here. Outside of faith, the hour is coming, for a consecrated Host does not look different from an unconsecrated one, but in faith everything that is promised already is. For the Lord, who was in the beginning with God, makes of everything that is beginning and is going to begin already its fulfillment. Beginning and fulfillment fall together. The Lord sees in our every attempt to begin already the accomplishment. And we see in all that he accomplishes a beginning. In every one of our movements, in every breath, every step of a man, the Lord sees a movement to himself and to the Father. And we see in every circle he closes, in every miracle he works, a beginning to something greater. Every grace he grants us is a beginning and an opening to greater grace, which we do not need to be conscious of and understand, as was the case with this one, but we are open to it, and so the grace received becomes in us the seed of a new grace that we are to receive. Every grace the Lord gives us is an absolute beginning, the beginning of something completely new. Today's Communion is an anticipation of that of tomorrow. The opening that takes place in every grace is an absolute one: like a point that opens to a thousand others, every one of which also opens out to a thousand others, and so infinitely. If someone has converted another to the Lord, this conversion would never be the end of the movement but becomes for both the starting point of a newly beginning infinite movement. No insight the Lord grants, no vision he may communicate, finds its end in itself, so that one could stay with it, but becomes at once the starting point of an infinite movement. What grace brings about is like a burning fire: a match is sufficient to kindle it; if it finds nourishment, it can go on burning infinitely, as is the nature of fire. An earthly fire can be quenched; the divine fire burning in faith is unquenchable insofar as it contains eternal life. Here, too, it is possible for life to be seemingly extinguished; a work of faith can be exteriorly prevented or destroyed; a mission station can be obliterated; a believer can be killed or imprisoned. But this does not touch the eternal life, which is pulsating in faith. All that lives and burns in the Lord is eternal life and eternal fire, alive and continuing to burn in the Lord. No one can say where this fire is spreading underground. If a work of faith is exteriorly destroyed, the flame of it remains at the Lord's further disposal; he can make use of it as he thinks best. The blood of the martyrs, for example, is fruitful visibly or invisibly, and every true obedience is likewise. But no man may for the sake of this invisibility forsake the exterior task entrusted to him. No one may strive for martyrdom as a goal; no one may give up a position he has been given to defend for the sake of a false heroism of obedience. And if the hour that now is is truly to be the one that is coming, the human factor of it must also always remain open to what is to come. For example, a religious could have begun a mission in the obedience of faith, but then the seed sown might be deprived of the opportunity of developing. The religious order might have too little faith and thus cut off every means of development for the work that has been begun, or the believer's obedience itself might cease to remain pure and open readiness before God. The hour must always be coming and be expected as such if it is to be the hour of the Lord that already is. Otherwise, the germinating seed planted into the earth would not in truth contain the whole plant but would be a dead seed.

That the hour is coming and already is has its ultimate ground in the being of the Son, who from all eternity, and so also in time, is ever and at once the one who has been sent and the one who is being sent. In this ultimate ground, the earthly truth is fulfilled that all that is coming is always already there: for while one man generates a child, another man dies or buries his child; while two become enkindled in love, love cools in two others. While on earth what is coming is already final and completed, in God what is coming is what is in movement from the world in eternal becoming. In the world, *the hour is coming, and now is* means that a circle is closed; in divine life, it is an infinite and open movement.

It is the hour *when the dead will hear the voice of the Son of God, and those who hear will live.* The dead the Lord here mentions are sinners. He is not speaking of bodily resurrection here. For the sinner the coming hour is here, because he can hear if he wants to. Those who hear will live in the eternal life of faith and in the eternal life of love. It is sufficient to hear in order to believe, to love, to live. Life appears as the highest here, because life is the fullness of faith, love, and hope. This life is present in what one hears, and what one hears is the content of the sacraments. These contain the word of the Lord insofar as it is eternal life. The voice of the priest administering the sacraments is the voice of the Lord—in quite a different and fuller sense than in preaching—for the Lord imparts through the priest's word in the sacrament the fullness of eternal life. The voice of the Lord that we hear when "Ego te absolvo a peccatis tuis" is said unbinds us from sin and gives us life simultaneously in a sacramental way. This sacramental word of the Lord leads the dead to life, and so the sacrament as word of the Lord contains in itself eternal life. On their journey through life, men receive this life ever anew, though it is eternal life. This is no contradiction, for if eternal life is one and undivided in eternity, in time there exist various degrees of intensity with which we share in eternal life. With some, one can hardly guess it; with others, it is an almost visible participation in eternal life. Some live here below and have a relationship to the beyond. Others live already in the beyond and share almost superficially and nonessentially in earthly life. The more life on earth becomes otherworldly, the more one needs the word of the Lord in the sacrament, as strengthening nourishment as well as a constant exhortation. As nourishment: the more fully one lives by the Lord, the more one is in need of his life. As exhortation: for no one is more in danger of mistaking what is from himself for what belongs to the Lord than the one who tries to live wholly in the Lord. Such a man needs to hear the Lord's word through the sacrament as often as possible, to rise each time more fully from death to self to the life of the Lord and allow one's earthly life to be changed into eternal life.

In this way, our life in faith, love, and hope needs to become attuned and conformed to the eternal life of the Lord in the sacrament. In the sacrament, the Lord is wholly eternal, uninterrupted life, touching our life here in space and time, so to say, only in tiny points and on the smallest basis. From these points, the Eucharist wants to draw us into the beyond, into the uninterrupted life of eternity. But because we are sinners, evil has the power to quench in us the eucharistic energy very quickly again. As sinners, we have the dangerous possibility of communicating frequently, perhaps daily, but allowing ourselves to be touched by eternity just for a moment; limiting Communion to a short preparation and thanksgiving but suffocating the eternal thanksgiving that is contained in the Eucharist, because we pin it down to our personal effort. We can get accustomed to looking at Holy Communion as a kind of courtesy call on the Lord, completed with the act of thanksgiving. We would then consider ourselves open to the Lord during a time set aside for it. But it would be a time remaining totally of this world, measurable, and unable to flow over into the immeasurable breadth of our life in the Lord. The Lord has shown us before that his love for the Father as thanksgiving is not tied to anything measurable, be it achievement, service, or return service; and the Eucharist is nothing else but the expression of this eternally streaming thanksgiving. In the sacrament, we are drawn into this very form of love. If the rest of our day, therefore, were to be excluded from our Communion, the latter could hardly be what it is meant to be. The reception of the Lord in Holy Communion may well be the climax of our day, but there must be no barrier separating it from the rest of the day, and this latter cannot be a turning away and separation from the Lord. The gift of Holy Communion and of the Lord's Real Presence in

THE CONFERRING OF JUDGMENT 189

the tabernacle certainly shows us a relationship the eternal Lord has with time and space, but no man is empowered to set a limit to these relations of the Lord and to narrow them down to a merely innerworldly presence in time and space. These points in time and space are "notches" that eternal life cuts into the flowing thread of our earthly life in order to find entry there. They are the expression of the Son's power over space and time but not a handle for us to control the Son in our time and space. We are of course allowed to use these "notches" ourselves; we may turn a visit to the Blessed Sacrament into a renewal of our daily life. But such a moment has at once to continue and go on working. Here, too, the unity of action and contemplation is asked for: what we have received is itself greater than our reception of it, so it must outlast the reception; we must not deprive it of the possibility of acting timelessly. The time of the Real Presence of the Lord outlasts all earthly time, and the place where the Host is reserved radiates to every spot in space. From these points, eternal life spreads like the fragrance of a flower; it does not remain enclosed within itself but pours itself out infinitely. This does not mean that the Lord's life in the world is not bound to his living word in the sacrament, but it means that, though bound to it, it has power over the world. It is precisely through the nothing of the Host that the eternal life of the Lord reaches into this earthly life; it is this nothing in terms of earthliness through which the tremendous greatness of the life beyond in faith and love is shown, symbolized, and revealed. We here below think we have true life, but the Lord here below chose the form of the Host, this insignificant frail nothing, in order to show us how much true life belongs to the beyond, the life that God immeasurably is in himself. And this life we are called to share. We should not try to confine it to the place where the mere symbol of it is. For it becomes alive in us only when even the symbol disappears, and we only carry and take it and allow it to work where it transcends us and streams over us. Earthly bread diminishes when someone feeds on it, but it is sufficient to look at the Lord to be nourished by him. And the more we behold him, the stronger becomes his effect on us; he does not diminish when we behold him, but through this beholding, his eternal life grows in us. For he contains it.

5:26. *For as the Father has life in himself, so he has granted the Son also to have life in himself.*

We have life, but not in ourselves. We receive it constantly anew from the hand of God. The Son, however, not only has life; he has it in himself. He is independent in his life; that is why he can appear in the world distinct from the Father. But his independence is of such a kind that he has his separate life always from the Father. Insofar as the Son is self-contained, he can pass on this life, which is at his disposal, to men. He passes it on in the way he himself possesses it: in eternally undiminished fullness, in the power that belongs to him as Son, in the superabundance that belongs to him as God. He gives it to us as he possesses it, for he regards us as sons of the Father and as his brothers. But he has it in such a way as to receive it eternally from the Father, and so he gives it to us also as a life received and accepted in gratitude and ever new to be received. We, however, do want life, but not to receive it as received in dependence and with gratitude.

The Father's self-giving in the Son is the origin of the Eucharist, the spring from which it flows. This first distribution in God in which the Father gives his whole being to the Son makes the infinite distribution of the Son in the world possible. The Son has not only received life from the Father; he has also accepted it, and exactly as accords with his mission as Son: in view of his own distribution in the world. And we also receive it according to our mission in the world as brothers of the Son. Our reception, however, remains sullied by sin; it will be according to the degree of our readiness a more or less powerful share in eternal life, which as our life remains life from beyond, a breath of eternal life breathing through our earthly life.

5:27. *And [he] has given him authority to execute judgment, because he is the Son of man.*

This authority to execute judgment that the Son receives at once exhausts itself because it becomes one with the authorization he is given to love. The authority to judge, seen in itself, would be the right to exact something from men. But the authority the Son receives is in reality the right to give them everything, that is, himself. So this judgment becomes the reverse of what anyone might expect. The sinner is not required to give something in doing penance, but he is authorized to take what the Lord gives him, his very self. The Lord has received this authority *because he is the Son of man.* For the second time we are meeting this name of the Lord. It is obscure, for we know of the Lord only that he is the Son of God; we do not know why he should be called Son of Man as a special distinction. But in truth that is what he is. He is the Son of the Most High and at the same time the son of the most lowly of men. He is the Son of him who has nothing to do with sin, and the son of him who is wholly bathed in sin. He is the Son of the Mother who was born without sin and gave birth without sin. But he is equally the son of the last and most abject of sinners. He is this because he has taken upon himself to become our neighbor. Our neighbor is the one nearest to us, who happens to stand beside us at any moment. It could be the mother, a brother or a friend, the teacher or pupil, or anyone at a meeting or in the street, or an enemy whom one does not want to meet at all but whom one accidentally encounters, or someone wholly unnoticed whom one does not see at all or overlooks or immediately forgets. It could be one with whom we have everything in common, who is one with us in faith, love, and hope; it could also be the one from whom everything divides us, who has neither faith nor love nor hope. It could be the one about whom we know everything and whom we completely understand, but equally the one wholly unknown to us, whom we shall never understand because we have no inclination to acquaint ourselves with his life, or because, in spite of honest endeavor, we shall never succeed in understanding him. It is especially of this one, the most beloved and the most hated, the one we seek and the one from whom we flee, the one we understand and the one who remains closed to us, it is especially of this one that Christ is the son. He *is* the Son: man as Son of God, and God as son of every man, of him who wants him and of him who does not want him; and so he becomes comprehensible to us as truly our neighbor and as truly Son of God. He is anonymous and at the same time the one who bears for us the most intimate name: our Lord. He is the one who bridges everything in the Father, because he embodies God in all men, and also as Son of Man he is the son of all and can be in all and so can point beyond the individual to God. The Lord's substance mediates between me and you, between every man and every other man. The Lord is not bound to a particular form of life, though he determines every form of life. He is in us in such a way as immediately to transcend us; he is also all around us, in our neighbor, where he lives in an equally essential and personal way, both fulfilling and transcending him as he does in us. In the Lord we find our neighbor's innermost reality and also his most ideal possibility, to which we are to lead him. Every man, therefore, is linked to God through the Son, and because the Son is in him, we also have to deal with the other in such a way that he comes to the Father in Christ. He is already placed within the movement from the Son to the Father. Through this fulfillment of our love of neighbor, the Lord is at the same time the fulfillment of our love of God. Without him, the Son of Man, God would remain far from us; we would know him only as spirit, not flesh, and our flesh would not be in relationship with him. In the Lord, however, we can adore God in the flesh we know and in this way gain access to the living Spirit. Because the Lord is our brother, we understand that God is our Father.

The movement of the Son toward the Father is timeless; that is why Christ is the Son also within time, and he is the Son of Man, the son of all men, because he is the Son par excellence and, so, the one who is always coming. He is the one toward whom life in time tends, in whom it reaches its goal, and in whom it is fulfilled. He is coming in an inseparably double sense; as the one coming from the Father and the one returning to the Father in the (eternal) future, on his way toward him. His sonship entails an enduring but ever-new, never completed movement, such as motherhood or brotherhood does not entail. In him, there always is the beginning of the movement, never the whole parabolic curve of it. A man's sonship begins with the first love of his parents, and it remains there in its origin. In the same way, the Father places into every man an original seed that opens out into a movement in which he goes through the Son to the Father. The Father distributes his own paternity among all mankind, so that everyone comes to share in the Father's fatherhood and thus becomes the father of the Son. In accord with this infinite distribution of the fatherhood among men, the Son also distributes and shares himself infinitely in the Eucharist, in which he as Son of God deigns to become also the son of men. And as the Son has life in himself by receiving it ever anew from the Father, so it is the mark of his truly being alive that in the world he ever comes into being in men. As with living, so it is the same with loving: love, if it is genuine, is always growing and becoming, never stationary, always striving, never coming to a limit that is not a new beginning.

As the Son of Man, therefore, the Lord judges in love. The question could arise why the Father did not judge in love in the Old Testament, since already he had then in himself the Son, whom he judges and loves from all eternity with a love that outstrips every justice. But the Old Covenant was the season of the Father's justice, and the Son's season of the judgment of love was reserved to the New Covenant. The reason is that this love could reveal itself in full perspective only in the Father's separation from the Son. Only in the sacrifice that lies in separation can love unfold its whole depth. It is the same in human love: only when the sacrifice has been made, or at least begun, can love fully show its power and blossom out. When about to sacrifice his son after having already interiorly made the renunciation, Abraham began to understand the love of God, having until then seen only his justice. God makes a sacrifice similar to that of Abraham. Abraham grasped the love of God for the first time on earth when out of love he did the biggest thing it was possible for him to do: he gave his dearest possession here below to the love beyond. The Father completes this sacrifice by giving his dearest possession from beyond in

THE CONFERRING OF JUDGMENT

sacrifice into this world here below. This act of God's love is meant to show us what love is and in what it consists. Both acts of sacrifice are similar to each other and are yet in contrast; in the first case, a man who sacrifices discovers in this sacrifice what love is; in the other case, men discover in the sacrifice the love of the one who sacrifices. It was in the Father's sacrifice that the inner love of God could reveal itself and become effective as the New Covenant. This Covenant is now an eternal one, while the Old Covenant was temporal. Abraham's sacrifice was a single act, perhaps done in the rapture of enthusiastic love. The Son, however, is surrendered by the Father to the world in an everlasting act, not in a summary way for all, but personally for each man. And the Son himself seals and augments the Father's sacrificial love for us by his own sacrifice. The sacrifice of the Cross is not an event that exhausts itself in the Lord's love for us; rather, it constrains the Father to a still greater love for us.

The Son as Son of Man is still the light in the darkness. That he is the Son coming from the darkness of humanity has its reason in the fact that he is the light. This light shines into our darkness, which resists it. In giving his Son to each one of us, the Father, like the Son in the Eucharist, gives us the opportunity of being judged by him in love and of being enabled in our turn to radiate what we have received. But we prefer the darkness to his love. He has abolished the judgment for us, so that we might be handed over to love. But we want judgment, not love. We prefer to be measured and weighed because we ourselves want to measure. We want to be praised or blamed within a world order familiar and accessible to us; we want to understand the judgment about ourselves and agree with it. As long as we ourselves do not love, we do not want to be subject to a judgment of love. We find this judgment of love unjust because it looks only to the criterion of love. It might happen that a big sinner who may have committed many sins, which we perhaps managed to avoid by means of great moral effort, is acquitted simply because he had love, while we, after accumulating a considerable treasure of virtues and moral achievements, are condemned merely because we accidentally did not have this virtue of love. We who have a sense of justice cannot accept such a judgment as just. But we do not realize that our sin lies precisely in this nonrecognition of the judgment of love. We would like to be our own advocates; we ask for a defense, a justification of the judgment given that would allow us to accept it and submit to it with good conscience. This means we want a true judgment, a restitution, justice. We do not want the love that goes beyond judgment. Our sense of justice would feel affronted if a sinner should fare better than ourselves in judgment. We are afraid of the unpredictability of this pure love. As darkness fears the light that conquers and destroys it, so we fear a love that overstretches our ego and enlarges the dimension of the you in us beyond the me in order to make us share in the relationship between Father and Son. We fear the life that God bears in himself; we seek security and order, and this precisely is darkness. We do not want this bigness in God himself and in our dealings with him or the surrender to a life that overwhelms us. We want the solitariness of our ego in spite of the longing we pretend to have; we do not want to be delivered up to the community. But if God allows every single one of us to possess his Son as our son, to be the men of the Son of Man, then he gives us the possibility of no longer suffering from loneliness and finding in the Son the community of all those who with us possess the mark of paternity. In making us his children, brothers of his Son, members of the Church, the Father inserts us

THE CONFERRING OF JUDGMENT

into his relationship with the Son: we are one not only in the Son, who returns to the Father, but also in the Father, who brings forth the Son. And this is what we fear, because we are afraid of love and life.

5:28. *Do not marvel at this; for the hour is coming when all who are in the tombs will hear his voice.*

Do not marvel: belong to me in such a way that you are open for what you do not understand. Give me your faith, like a child; take from my hands whatever comes; take it, whatever it may be, with thanksgiving, not with questions; with hunger, not mistrust; ready for the whole gamut of possibilities, without calculating. One who marvels, criticizes, compares is overly occupied with what he already knows, possesses, and has experienced, with what he is, what his reason can accept as valid, rather than with the wholly new and original that God offers. One who is open for God cannot marvel at anything. If he marvels, he shows that he is occupied with himself rather than with God. One living in God is so powerfully aware that God always transcends everything and surpasses all expectations that every comparison with anything that has been before is already silenced. Wonderment is the beginning of doubt and unbelief because it is the beginning of self-opinionatedness.

For the hour is coming when all who are in the tombs will hear his voice. They are not to marvel at events they can least expect and believe, which are not in any way part of their experience. The Lord does not say: do not marvel even though . . . ; he explicitly states, for . . . all this is coming. It is coming and will surpass you because it will be the work of God. Therefore surrender to it right from the beginning. Marveling would mean stopping and drawing limits. But to go forward and drop all defenses is the right thing to do here. In such a way that nothing, not even the most unexpected is capable of ever robbing you of your love of God. Not even what is most unlikely, which is that the dead *who are in the tombs will hear his voice.*

5:29. *And come forth, those who have done good, to the resurrection of life, and those who have done evil, to the resurrection of judgment.*

This division cuts sharply through everything said so far. It was said that the judgment of justice was to be replaced by that of love. So the first part is familiar to us: the identification of judgment with love and eternal life. And yet those who have done good will be separated from those who have done evil. The separation is as complete as though men could really be sharply divided into those who have done good and those who have done evil. As if they were not all darkness and did not all repeatedly say No to the light. So this sudden absolute division becomes an inexplicable conundrum to us. Yet Abraham was shown to us as one who was ready to make the sacrifice God was asking. There really exists a readiness to sacrifice. The possibility exists of opening oneself to what one does not understand. The possibility of surrender exists. What is expected of those who do good is no more than readiness. Those who do evil are those who are in no way ready to sacrifice, who do not try at all to open themselves to love, to be receptive for the love of neighbor, the love of God. Those who do evil do no more than simply refuse to surrender. Among those who do good, all variations and degrees are possible. They may really share in love and give themselves eucharistically with the Lord. It is also possible that they have given at some time a weak and hardly audible consent to some kind of love, the love of the Lord or of neighbor, or to any offer, however slight, as long as it takes place within love. These degrees do not exist among those who do evil. They are the ones who simply and always say No and are solely occupied with ever saying No in order not to give in to the temptation to think a Yes even for a short moment. They do not want to know any love other than self-love. These will come forth to the resurrection of judgment.

So there is a judgment after all. We are confronted with a paradox. We just heard that the Father has given all judgment to the Son and that the Son is able to give life and so redemption, love, to all to whom he wishes to give it. There are no barriers set to his wishes. But now we do see a barrier. That the Lord pushes the barrier of evil as far away as possible corresponds to his role as Redeemer, and it might look as if these absolute refusers are really the limit in such a way that they really do not exist. But the Lord does not say this. The Father has given all judgment to him, not to us. What he shows us is the possibility of a judgment with two different outcomes.

5:30. *I can do nothing on my own authority; as I hear, I judge; and my judgment is just, because I seek not my own will but the will of him who sent me.*

The Lord has just said that the total judgment belongs to him, as a judgment of love. God has handed to him the authority to judge because he is the Son of Man. Wherever he is not the Son of Man (*des Menschen*), he does not have this authority to love and pass the judgment of love. Because men share in the fatherhood, it is up to them to decide whether they want him to be the Son. He stands there, so to say, with hands bound, waiting for those whom he is to judge, waiting also for those who do evil. These are the ones to whom it has not been given to acknowledge him as their son. Those who do so place themselves under the judgment of love. The Son cannot do anything on his own authority because he can do only what he sees the Father doing, and the Father's condition for the judgment of love is that his Son should also be the Son of Man. He was sent by the Father under this condition, and outside of it he can do nothing because only under this condition he can be what he is: the Son. Those who have the Son as son are those of whom it was said (in verse 27) that they have a neighbor and know him. These form the community of those who accept the Son and do good. The Son can do nothing on his own authority. For as Son he is bound to the Father and to us, to this double paternity, this double origin.

As I hear, I judge. Hearing, he hears as the Son, and this as the Father's Son and as Son of Man. He listens in both directions. He must constantly listen to whether his divine Sonship and his human sonship are linked together. He listens to whether there is something in the life of the one to be judged that fits into this relationship of love, that has been taken up into his living love, or can be taken up, or at least could be as a possibility of faith, something at all that is capable of love.

My judgment is just, because I seek not my own will but the will of him who sent me. God has sent him out of love on a mission of love. He has sent him, therefore, with a particular intention under a particular condition, as far as his mission and his Sonship are concerned. The judgment will be passed in no way other than within these relations willed by the Father. The Lord does not say anything beyond this; he does not indicate what he does with those he judges; he does not exclude the possibility of all being finally judged in the judgment of love, in his own judgment. It is not part of his mission to reveal this to mankind.

Even less does he say that he will save those who do not have love. He abruptly finishes his speech. If we were all sure that we are to be judged in the judgment of love, our love would go to sleep. The possibility of a different judgment enkindles in us love for the Lord. He separates the good from the bad. The good are judged in love. He says of the bad that he will judge them also, for the whole judgment has been given to him. And here he breaks off. He has almost said too much already. He hands everything back to the Father, places the judgment into the Father's hands. He entrusts his will to the Father in order to finalize the content of his mission in this abrupt movement upward, and those who belong to him in the Father recognize through this movement that he is, after all, love to the end.

THE TESTIMONY

5:31. *If I bear witness to myself, my testimony is not true.* With these words, the Lord, of course, cannot mean that there is any way in which he does not speak the truth. He can want to say only that he would not speak the truth if he were to bear witness to himself. If he were a mere man like the others and as such were to bear witness to himself, then his testimony would not be true.

Yet God does demand a *testimony* from every man. In creation, God has spoken a word that calls for an answer. God has given a testimony of himself to man and demands in return a testimony from man; he must bear witness to his own truth. He cannot renounce this testimony, and he never does. No sinner is forsaken or given up by God; to the last, God demands his return and so the clarification of the situation between the sinner and himself. He demands a testimony, and this testimony has to contain the absolute, decisive truth and answer of the creature to God; God cannot be content here with the conventional, compromised, and indecisive truth that men are wont to exchange.

But man in himself is unfit to bear such a testimony to himself. As man, he knows two kinds of truth. The first is what he knows through his sense experience to be true, all that his senses tell him. But this truth is relative to his own subjective self and unfit to serve as foundation for an objective testimony. He can bear witness to the taste of some food: he finds it too sweet. But the same food will be too sour for another. He could not foresee this, and even if he knows it, he can never explain it. The sphere of an individual's sense experience is subjective and unexchangeable. Even the highest love between men cannot break through this barrier between two persons. A wife may be taking a lot of trouble in preparing the meal according to her husband's taste, but she will never come to know how it actually tastes to him. There is no bridge here from me to you and, so, no truth. What a man says of himself in this sphere concerns himself only; he can state his preferences and his aversions, but even he himself cannot look into the foundation on which his evaluation is based. His taste can change. Ultimately, he cannot explain himself on this level; were he to speak ever so explicitly about himself and to describe his experiences as objectively as possible from various points of view, he would never be able to convey to another what he really experiences and feels, how a particular color touches him, how some fruit has tasted to him.

Besides these truths experienced by the senses, men know various kinds and degrees of general truths about which they converse and for the sake of which they dialogue and enter into intellectual exchange. These are truths of everyday life, more or less generally agreed on. Though these truths are not dependent on the individual's personal experience, for that very reason they are not suitable, either, for stating anything essential and decisive about him as person. They do not even touch on his personal identity, his ultimate destiny. Therefore, they do not enable him to bear a true witness to himself.

The truth with which a man is able to operate in daily life is so thin and precarious that it does not permit him to bear witness to himself before God, before ultimate and absolute truth. He would be enabled to do this only if God were to give him access to this eternal truth himself, if man were enabled to bear his witness and give his answer in the word in which he exists in the beginning with God, in which he was created and which remains with God. The precarious character of all innerworldly truth calls on man to transcend the witness of his own senses and conventional judgments, to hear his own real truth from God himself, and to surrender it back to God in his answer. But because man is not willing to do this, because he attempts to bear a testimony from his own self, he falls into sin. Sin consists in the refusal to accept his truth from God and give it back to him and in wanting to possess it for himself. This attempt to remain in one's own truth is untruth and a lie. As long as man remains in this state, every attempt to express his own truth and give a testimony of himself will be the expression of a lie. Even when he is talking in terms of generally accepted truths, these are used in the service of a lie and are an expression and in function of a lie. They serve as a coverup before God and before oneself so as not to have to look one's own truth in the face. Such a testimony has an ulterior motive and color. The sinner does not see himself as he truly is in this testimony; his sin prevents it. The sin exists precisely in this endeavor not to face up to oneself as one truly is. On the surface, the sinner is ready to bear any witness desired. But he does not want to lay his interior open, his inmost center and being. He uses his testimony as a coverup. The more voluble he is in talking about himself, the less he wants to expose his own interior. He tries to distract others from the real question with a spate of half-truths that are mere lies. If these half-truths are not conventional truths, they depend wholly and entirely on the subjective experience of the individual. The sinner never stops bearing witness to these. His sensuality provides him with sensations that he mistakes for personal experiences, and so he believes that in expressing them he bears witness to his own truth. But all he witnesses to is his self-centeredness: his refusal to live in the truth. God asks a total witness of man; the man is to appear naked before him. The sinner is ready to give any testimony apart from this unique and total one. He is ready to uncover one side of his being after another, as long as he can keep the others covered in the meantime. He fears nothing so much as the fundamental diagnosis; he is quite ready to confess the symptoms of his illness and receive treatment for them. He shies away from a total view of his state and believes that if it remains vague to himself, it will remain so to God, also. His hope is that God then will forget about asking the one great question that can be answered, not with a thousand partial answers, but with only one single word. He also is afraid that God could take advantage of his testimony. He agrees that God is entitled to ask a total witness of others, priests, religious, and some laymen. This witness of others, of "the Church", should be so convincing and spectacular that his own would be superfluous. He would need only to point to the official testimony of the Church if anyone should demand a witness from himself. The others ought to bear the total testimony. But as far as he himself is concerned, compromise is the only thing he knows.

The testimony God demands of man is a total one. It is therefore a witness in word and in life and the unity of both. If word and life are divergent from each other, if one of them does not correspond to the truth, it would then not be the witness of the total person. It is not difficult for one who knows the truth of God to bear witness to it in words. But this witness will reach its full truth only when it falls together with the witness of one's life. If a man does not live the truth he proclaims, he will not come across as himself convinced and so will not be convincing. To give a testimony of the truth in words is easy; it is difficult to do so by one's life. For a man remains a sinner who can never perfectly express the truth of God in his life. Also, the witness of life, when it is given, is one of simplicity, perhaps a hidden one; without the sensational that belongs to a witness in words, it is therefore not equally unmistakable. The witness of life lends itself to quite different interpretations. Different motivations can be attributed to it; it can be read by each one as he chooses. Even the truest witness can be untruthful when it is received by sinners who misinterpret it. In this sense, even the Lord's witness before the Jews falls short of the truth. They do not accept his testimony given in words, because they thirst for the sensation of his deeds; neither do they accept the witness of his life, for it accuses them. They judge it according to their own motivation, their own subjectivity, and their general and compromised conventions. The testimony they receive is quite different from the one the Lord gives. They project their own attitudes into him. Every true witness of the Christian life has to suffer this. It does not give a true testimony because people do not want to accept it as such, and so they even are incapable of receiving it. Even if a man sincerely tries to bear a true witness by allowing his words to be borne out by his life, this testimony would not be true because it is not accepted as true. People would criticize his words because they do not correspond with his life, or they criticize his life because it does not speak a word loud enough for them not to misinterpret it.

There is only *one* possibility of bearing an ultimate and true witness, which is to bear witness to the absolute truth of absolute truth. The absolute truth about ourselves exists only in God, ordained and administered by him. We get to know it only in faith. In faith alone can man learn the truth about himself. This truth is that as long as he refuses to see himself through faith in God, he is a sinner; but as soon as he takes hold in faith of the truth of God, his sin is separated from him. Even in faith, however, he cannot see himself in the truth in such a way that he has a complete overview of his truth. Even when he sees with God's eyes, he can see only the one aspect of this truth. He either sees himself as one held captive by sin and encompassed with a lie: then he sees, not the sin itself, but its effect in the sinner. Or he sees himself somehow separated from his sin (at the moment when he bears witness to his sin before God, for example): he loses sight of what he looks like connected with his sin. Even in faith, therefore, man remains dependent on what God says about him. He does not judge and witness to his own self in faith; otherwise, even his witness in faith would be untrue. He bears witness only to what he hears in faith to be God's witness to him. This testimony that God gives is the truth about man. For man is essentially what God makes him and continues to make him and not what he believes himself to be. What a man is in truth is decided by the way God looks at him, which, thanks to the Son, is a look of love and not of justice. And this testimony God gives, which we make our own in faith, receives its full truth when it is given back to God, the absolute truth. If it were given only to the world, to man, or to the believer himself, it would not be accepted as a true testimony and would not have the character of absolute truth.

A fully valid testimony, therefore, can be given only by one who comes from eternal truth and returns to eternal truth; the Son of the eternal Father. For he bears witness, not to himself—otherwise it would not be true—but to the Father, from whom he comes; and he bears this witness ultimately, not to the world, which does not accept it, but to the Father, to whom he returns. Even when bearing witness to himself, which, because of his mission, he has to do, he does so only as the Son sent by the Father. Because of this, the eternal truth of the Father bears witness to itself in him. Every other testimony given by men must therefore be given within this testimony of the Son. It can claim to be truth only insofar as it is, as testimony by word or life, within the way of the Son.

The sinner's witness lies outside this way. His testimony by word is always a false one because it is nourished by sin and is directed toward sin. It is a lie, because if sin looks at itself in sin, it can only result in a lie. Even the sinner's lived testimony is a lie. His action remains within sin and is subject to sin. The testimony God asks of him is first of all to stop sinning. But the sinner is unwilling to do this.

The testimony of the Christian is the attempt to bear witness within the Lord's testimony. His testimony by word is the attempt to bear witness directly to the word of God in Christ. He embarks on this attempt in spite of knowing himself to be a sinner. He places the whole of his own darkness into the light of the Lord's testimony. He does not stop short with the darkness, though it exists and is true. He turns away from the truth of this darkness in order to turn toward the truth of the light of Christ and to speak in the name of the Lord of this light. The testimony could stand in the light of the Lord without being accepted by sinners. These would seek in it only an expression of their sin, would make a synthesis or conglomeration of what they see as their own testimony and what the Christian sees as his own witness within that of the Lord. The Christian's testimony could have been given in the light of the Lord and as such be true but could at the same time have been accepted by sinfulness and as such be untrue.

The Christian can also try to bear witness to the truth by deed. He can try to live in God. His deeds would then be the expression of this attempt. If it is done within faith and love, the sin would be secondary; the direction of his life is moving away from sin to the light of the Lord. It will be an attempt and never be anything more. By himself, the Christian will never succeed in making his testimony completely one with his existence. But he is dragging the sinner he is toward the light of God, and so the sinner becomes secondary; important and primary is the light alone toward which he is turned. Even the sinner thus being dragged along becomes an instrument offered to the Lord for his use. It is no longer this particular sinner who is placed at the Lord's disposal; a kind of neutralization takes place: in the testimony that is being lived out, the Lord's instrument and his work are being brought together and become a true unity. Sinners, however, will not accept this existential Christian witness, either. They project their own actions into those of Christians and seek the place where they touch each other in sin. In the objective appearance of such deeds, there are many such points of convergence, which did not exist in the purely subjective sphere of sense and taste. In space and time, all actions meet each other, though their true motives are hidden. In this objective sphere, it is possible to misinterpret the lived testimony of Christians and explain it in the direction of sin.

The Christian testimony can be given only within the perfect testimony of the Lord. The Lord himself bears witness in word and life. Each of his words is a total, indivisible, and absolute testimony that comes from the Father and goes to the Father and desires to draw men into this movement. For that is its purpose, to give men the opportunity of moving alongside it to God. But this testimony of the Lord is not accepted. Unbelievers hear in it only what he does not say, which is what their own sin inspires them with. Believers also color the testimony according to their capacity of receiving. They make it relative where it is intended to be absolute. They, too, have not learned how to hear it as it is said. Not only do they never grasp the word in all its vastness or hear it in the perfect purity and love in which it was expressed, but they still imagine that they can hear and understand this testimony as independent and equal partners with God. They themselves want to determine its meaning, content, competence, and limits. They accept only part of the testimony offered, not only in fact, but also in full consciousness. They accept it as something in itself complete whereas it is given only to lay them open to God. They accept it as a result accomplished when all it wants is to begin a movement that is to take them to God. The Lord's testimony is so expressly addressed to the Christian in the Christian that he hardly comprehends it. The sinner in him stands in the way. We can hear his truth and accept his testimony only when we really hear it in faith, when it is no longer the finite man but grace in us, the child of God in us, that hears. God's testimony can be heard only in God. And even here our hearing remains inchoate.

The Lord's testimony is also a lived testimony. His actions speak as loudly as his words. His works and miracles bear witness to his origin. These deeds wholly transcend us and launch us powerfully into God's truth. They are more difficult to understand than the word that is proclaimed. The word adapts itself to the human mind; it is echoed in the soul. The deed, in contrast, sweeps us up and pulls us after itself. It shakes the whole person, not only the ear. This is the case more particularly when the testimony of deeds and miracles becomes the testimony of suffering. Here the Lord's witness overwhelms us, converts us; it effects in the Christian who sees and understands it a kind of reversal, turning him inside out, a sore, a cataclysm that propels him to God with the force that belongs to the Lord in his Passion. This is a testimony that grips and takes hold of a person so that he loses sight of where he is drawn. He begins to run to God and stops asking whether he himself is running or is dragged along. Through the grace of the Lord, the testimony has become such obvious truth that only running counts, and it ceases to matter whether it is active or passive. The testimony of the Lord hits the Christian, not as a separate and independent person, but as one who is taken along and who must follow, like a question taken into the word of God that the Lord himself answers. Here, in the Passion, the Lord's testimony is true even for the world, because the Lord's power confers the stamp of truth on it. His truth becomes forcibly manifest in a way that cannot be further resisted. The truth of the Passion, which the Lord explains to the believer, has the power of carrying him along. It is a work of love. But it is this only for the believer (and that the world comes to believe is the fruit of the testimony of the Passion); for unbelievers, Christ's deeds, like his words, will serve only as an occasion to project their own selves into them and to interpret them according to the norm of their own sin.

The testimony of the Lord is and remains a testimony from God, in God, and for God. God asks a testimony from everyone, but from no one as urgently as from the Son. From him he asks an absolute testimony. He demands it because he knows he will receive it. In spite of this, he cannot renounce asking it, for the asked-for testimony is one with the absolute testimony contained from the beginning in the mutual love of Father and Son. The Son's testimony embraces his entire life on earth; every contemplation, every act in it, is a testimony to the Father. It is an answer to him before any question has been raised, an answer lying ready from eternity, anticipating any question. The Father never needs to ask a question without being sure beforehand that the answer is already given; he already sees it before him. The Christian is permitted to grow into this perfect testimony of the Son. Every Christian testimony that looks only to the Lord and keeps only his testimony in view is a true testimony. It is a testimony that has its perfection in the Lord and preexists in him and is called "ours" only because we are permitted through grace to grow into this perfection. The Lord's testimony is the only true testimony, because it is true always and forever. We who try to model our witness on his are true for only seconds at a time. He is the perfect mirror of the Father. In us there is from time to time a shimmer of it. We move away from the life of truth through sin. But the Son is even in death and in godforsakenness the perfect testimony to the Father's love.

5:32. *There is another who bears witness to me, and I know that the testimony which he bears to me is true.*

The *other* to whom the Son here refers is the Father as well as John the Baptist. John bears witness, and his testimony is true; he is the model of those who bear witness in God. He has received a mission from God, and within this mission he bears witness to the Lord. That is why his testimony is true. He is the first example and the archetype of the man bearing witness. His whole existence constitutes his testimony. He witnesses before he is born. He is awakened to this testimony by the Mother of the Lord; his leap in his mother's womb is not only a miracle but already an explicit testimony. Though he is human and therefore a sinner, his testimony is absolutely true. For he bears witness, not to himself, but to the Lord. He comes on the scene only to point away from himself to the Lord. He cannot be left out of the work of salvation of Father and Son, for this work needs the human witness to complete the divine testimony. It is very necessary that he should be already there before the Son himself. But he is a true witness only within the testimony of the Lord.

The Father also is the other who bears witness to the Lord. His testimony is all-embracing and begins already long before the Son himself appears: in the promises of the Old Testament. Later, the Father gives a testimony to him in Mary's conception and most clearly in allowing the Son to live his life as Son on earth. He accompanies the Son so closely on his way that he allows no separation from himself to occur. Though the Son lives on earth and the Father remains in heaven and the distinction between them is evident, yet both live in each other. So the Father is always acting with the Son in his mission: even the separate work of the Son is a work and testimony of the Father. When a man sends another to accomplish a task, the one commissioned can try to carry out the task in love according to the plan of the one who sent him. He can make this plan his own as best he can and try to adapt himself to it. But there will always be a discrepancy between the task and its execution. But there is not the slightest divergence between Father and Son. The testimony the Son gives to the Father is identical with the testimony the Father gives to the Son. On the basis of the Father's testimony to him, the Son also has to witness to himself. He does so, not as mere man, or his testimony would not be true. He does it as the Son who bears witness to himself as the one to whom the Father has borne witness. He bears witness to himself, not as person, but as the one sent (see 8:33ff.). In word and deed, he bears witness to himself as the promised Redeemer of the world, and this is his testimony. He has done it before; he will do it again; it belongs to his vocation. His mission obliges him to bear witness to himself. Unceasingly he points to his way: where he comes from and where he is going, to the road from the light of the Father into the darkness of the world and back to the Father's light. As the Father's living testimony, he bears witness to himself. Everyone to whom another has borne witness has to add his own testimony. So also the Christian in the following of Christ. His Christian mission obliges him to this. The Christian witness to oneself is twofold. First of all, it witnesses to the fact that the one who gives testimony has been graced. He knows in faith what he has received from God: faith, grace, and his mission. This constitutes his existence before God. He bears witness to it as a Christian. His arguments are no longer human but Christian arguments. But they do not bypass the human person or the witnessing person. John bound his disciples first to himself through his testimony in order to give them afterward to the Lord. In the same way, any witness points to his own testimony in order to draw the attention of others to the content of this testimony, which is Christ. But the witnessing Christian is particularly called upon to give testimony when this latter cannot come across as true. In the instant it is effective, fully accepted as true, it ceases to be necessary. It is necessary before sinners, to whom it appears first of all incomprehensible and abstract, who are quite unwilling to accept it as a true testimony. It is necessary where, combined with the testimony of the Lord's Passion, it helps to overcome the darkness of sin, through the power of this Passion and rejection. As soon as resistance is removed, the Christian is no longer required to bear witness in words. His deeds are speaking for him and absolve him from the obligation of showing his mission also in words. The Lord, however, testifies to himself, for he is the eternal and eternally living Word.

There is another testimony man has to give in the Lord. As a seal of his promise and of the truth of his redemption in us, the Lord has obliged us to bear another witness, which is that of bearing witness to one's sin in confession before his representative. This required testimony is, of course, a very limited one, something like the negative of a positive testimony. We are to confess and bear witness to our darkness so that he can bear witness to his own light in us. These two testimonies are not of equal value, do not correspond to one another. Our testimony is only an attempt to open ourselves to the light, a powerless attempt made in the darkness. It cannot be the truth or bring it about. The Lord in demanding it does not allow it to be true; he allows its truth to appear only for an instant in order to make it at once disappear again as untruth in his absolution. The sin that I confess is true; my sorrow may also be true, and the desire I have to recognize my sin and try to confess it in God's light. But at the moment itself when this truth appears, at the moment when my sorrow and my attempt to be true express themselves, grace is already there and dissolves and consumes this truth. My action cannot be undone. But it disappears in this light and becomes effectively as if it had never happened. Had I murdered ten people and then gone to confession, the ten corpses would still be there, but it would no longer be true that I am a murderer. The sinner in me has murdered them, but the Lord has removed this very sinner from myself in his forgiving. And that is why man's testimony to himself is never true, because he cannot exclude from it or include in it the effect of grace, which transforms everything. He has no control over it, no general view. At the moment when he can no longer stand himself or bear with himself because a dawning of the truth has taken hold of him and he bears witness to it, this witness ceases to be true because it is submerged in the forgiving love of the Lord.

In confession, the Christian bears witness in the Lord to what he is without the Lord. But this also he can see only with the Lord's eyes, the eyes of truth, when he is in the Lord. His confession of sin is not a testimony of man to himself. This would not be a true one. Rather, the truth of this testimony is enclosed in the truth of the Lord. In confession, man turns away from his untruth, which is his sin, in order to open himself to the light of the Lord's truth.

Man can speak to God also in silence, because he has been created in the word, and nothing has been created without the word. In confession, too, he bears witness not only through what he says but also through what he does not say. He may not knowingly hold anything back; but as soon as he endeavors to say everything, he becomes aware that he is at the same time confessing things that remain unsaid and are unsayable. The very fact that he stands there going to confession says more than he can express in words. Each individually formulated self-accusation contains something more that is unexpressed. For even in confession, it is more the Lord who bears witness than the sinner. The half-truth of the sinner is backed by the whole truth of the Lord, who knows all about the sin and stands in for the confession. Both priest and penitent are taken into a work of Christ that transcends them; each becomes a part of Christ's life without being able to see how it happens or how grace is working. They participate in the meeting of the Redeemer with the redeemed: however personal the sacrament of confession is to the individual sinner, the grace of confession transcends him and reaches beyond him into the pure sacramental event of the Church.

5:33. *You sent to John, and he has borne witness to the truth.* Those who sent to John demanded a testimony from him; they were convinced that he could give it. For this they themselves had to be in a state of knowing that truth exists, even though it implies nothing more than that. They were in this position because as Jews they had the promises. And they received what they asked for because John's testimony was that he is not the Messiah. John could tell them the truth because as the one commissioned it was his task to bear witness to it. Everybody who has a mission from God and understands it can bear witness to the truth about himself. Mission and witness are one because they are one in God.

Christ possesses the truth. John bears witness to it. Men seek it. Those who seek the truth seriously come so close to it that they are in the truth at least in the field of their own mission and can bear witness to it with John. They are sinners, but their sin, which might prevent them being in the truth, can become so secondary, so much given over to God, that they can be true in their mission and within their task. In confession, the sinner tries to put himself in the state of being able to hear God's forgiving word. This redeeming word places the sinner in the truth. Something similar takes place in a mission. God cannot suffer an untruth in the act of forgiveness; neither can he suffer an untruth in the act of mission. In the measure in which a man, though a sinner, lives within his mission, he lives in the truth. The mission is his truth before God; life within his mission is like an ongoing confession, for one who has been sent has to live and act as if only his mission were his reality. In his mission, he does not stand for himself but represents the one who sent him. And this one is the truth. Confession and mission belong together. In confession, man bears witness by accusing himself. In the mission, he bears witness by praising God without speaking of himself. Both aspects become one truth, the confession of sin and the confession of grace. Confession of sin is made in and through grace, and every grace is related to a mission.

5:34. *Not that the testimony which I receive is from man; but I say this that you may be saved.*

The Lord is not in need of a human testimony, for he is with God and in God, and there also man's truth is to be found. Even when a man's testimony is true, and especially when it is true, his truth is not in the testimony but in God. And God is not dependent on human testimony as the form of revealing his truth. He can use it if he wants to. He can let his light shine in the darkness, where no men are present; but he is equally free to let his light shine among men through men. He is free to radiate it in himself in his eternal solitude and also free to draw men into this radiation of eternal light.

But I say this that you may be saved. What does he say? That the truth is in God. That man must confess his sin for grace and truth to become effective. And he says this *that you may be saved.* That is the result of this whole statement about confession and mission. All this is redemption. For redemption consists in this: to be freed from one's sin and to be given a place in the mission toward life. Both together make up one truth. This truth, therefore, has a double aspect and is one because of this: truth as the continually renewed act of absolution in confession and as the once forever given, all-embracing act of the Lord's mission and our mission in him. Confession gives the Christian the opportunity of receiving absolution every day if he so wishes or at certain intervals fixed by himself. But he can also be absolved in a timeless, continuous way through his life within his mission, independent of his choice in time.

THE TESTIMONY

In between these two poles of truth, a third reality exists that unites them: the Christian year, the Church's year. At the appointed times, for example, in Eastertide, when the Christian is obliged to receive the sacraments, the great timeless absolution enters into the wheel of earthly time. God leaves every Christian the greatest personal freedom in choosing the manner in which to live his life of faith but also sets limits to this freedom by fitting it into a certain ecclesial structure. The urgency of the call to Easter duties recalls the great redemption and reminds us of the fact that the sacraments we can receive daily are the expression of this great redemption, which has been achieved once and for all. The Church accepts the most varied possibilities of living and expressing the Christian life. She has among her members people who live the sacramental life totally in and from their mission. Others are being lifted up ever again through the reception of the sacraments to the heights of their mission, from which they would otherwise sink down. Others, each time they receive, will recognize again something of this mission and take hold of it; finally, there are those whom the Church must constantly exhort to the reception of the sacraments and who have to be dragged there in some way. But all forms of the Christian life are found together in the Church as Spouse of Christ and Mediatrix between Christ and Christians, between the personal sphere of the freedom of Christ and the personal sphere of the freedom of individual Christians. In this role as Mediatrix, she cannot wholly renounce the character of the impersonal, even rigid officiality. In this way alone can she join the two spheres and coordinate them. So the Church is of necessity structured and hierarchical. This very officiality is the surest guarantee that she has the Holy Spirit, who is the Spirit of Christ. In the Holy Spirit, the Christian's spirit submits to and fits itself into the Spirit of

Christ. The Holy Spirit is the Spirit of the true personal freedom of both God and man, but this freedom consists in the mission to men, and every mission is an office and demands obedience. The Christian order is the coordination of the missions. The Church has the task of pasturing her sheep; she may not abandon them to some arbitrary private life with Christ; this would not be a Christian life. She exhorts them and does so through the order of the sacramental life. Precisely in this official side of her liturgy, the interior life of the Spouse of the Lord is safe and hidden, ever anew conforming itself to the Bridegroom's life in order to live with him and through him and share in his divine life.

5:35. *He was a burning and shining lamp, and you were willing to rejoice for a while in his light.*

John the Baptist stands here as the model and representative of any saint. He makes clear that the saint's meaning is to be a signpost to the Lord and that he meets with a tragic misconception in the Church. The saint burns. And because he burns, he shines and radiates light. The light that he radiates is the Lord's fire, for it is only in this fire that he shines and burns. He enlightens and warms the world with the fire of Christ; it is his mission to attract people to this luminous glow of the Lord and set them afire themselves. But people are willing to rejoice for only an hour, a short while in this light. The time is so short that they cannot catch fire themselves, and so the lamp remains ineffective. They fear the consequences; they do not want to burn themselves; they like to keep the saint as an image above them but not as a model beside them. They prefer to have nothing to do with the love that consumes him. They dread becoming burned out. At heart they seek something that will quench rather than enkindle them. They have hardly caught a glimpse of this love when they are already convinced that they have the whole. And every spark causes the worst fears to rise in them, because they do not understand that the Lord when he lights the flame will also guard it. So they are all the more forced to misinterpret the meaning of the light. They are well aware that John spreads a radiance, a light and warmth, but they do not want to attribute this light and warmth to the Lord, from whom it comes and to whom it leads. They choose to limit the light and confine it to the human person of John. This allows them to make a limited surrender to it: they offer him a little while of their precious time. They erect a double barrier: they limit the saint's light as well as the time they are prepared to spend looking at it. Instead of looking at the light itself, they pay attention to the lamp, which is of less importance. A lamp is at the service of the light. And especially when the light is the Lord himself, the lamp is only an unimportant instrument for it. If the lamp is to fulfill its mission, both barriers must be removed; only then can the light freely shine and be accepted in its fullness. That is why John is a paradigm of the saints: if he were the light himself, he might be a "man of stature", a "religious genius". But he would not be a saint. He would be something in himself, but the saint is an instrument of the light, nothing more.

5:36. *But the testimony which I have is greater than that of John; for the works which the Father has granted me to accomplish, these very works which I am doing, bear me witness that the Father has sent me.*

The Jews received John's testimony first, knowing that he burns. But the Lord has a greater testimony. He says, not I *give* a greater testimony, but I *have* a greater testimony. He has it in himself; he is the testimony. The light of this testimony is the absolutely greater and cannot be limited to any hour or time; it surpasses every measure. He does not say how great it is. He says only *greater*. He does not use a superlative but uses a comparative, which, however, is infinite and, so, the true superlative. For the Lord surpasses everything; he has no norm above him; he knows of no limitation. Every question about him will always call forth the answer: I am greater. This greater can never be comprehended, because it is still greater than everything that has ever been comprehended, and all comparisons fade before this eternal superlative. He is ever-greater. If we were to ask the Lord who he is, the answer would be: I am more. If we were to ask: What do you want of me? the answer would be: I want more. He is the being that is ever-greater and, therefore, a demand ever on the increase. The more that he attributes to himself contains the more that he has to demand from us. But while he *is* more, we must *become* more. And the greater our increase (if we are really growing), the higher he appears above us, as the one who always *is* already more. The more clearly we understand what he says, the more we also understand that he is more than we can understand and the greater becomes the demand on us to become more ourselves, because we know that he always wants to give us more than we can hold today. We can participate in his *state* of *being* more only when we remain in the *life of becoming* more. This does not mean that he is the being in rest, and we the becoming in the flux of life. For he has said of himself that he is the life. This flowing life, which he is in himself, is the same as the infinite increase, the Ever-Greater. But for him it means *being* more and, for us, participating in this by *becoming* more. When he says of John that he is a burning and shining lamp, he is saying that John is alive with the life of ever becoming more, for his life consists in radiating ever more life, and this life is the Lord and is therefore the Ever-Greater.

The greater testimony that the Lord here claims consists in the *works* he does as the one sent by the Father. They witness to him and his mission. This gift of the Father to him is a double one: it is made up of the *works* the Father gives him to achieve and the *grace* to achieve them. These works therefore belong first to the Father, who gives them to the Son to do. And secondly, they are the works of the Son, and the Father's gift is that of allowing him to do them as his own. In the first aspect, he is the one the Father has sent fulfilling his mission in the world by doing the Father's works. In the other aspect, he himself works freely as the one who freely gave his assent to the Father. This shows us the difference between the Son's mission and that of an ordinary man. When God chooses someone to give him a mission, he first of all asks for his assent and then entrusts him with the mission. He needs this quasi-unconditional assent before he can give a particular mission. So it was with Mary. With the Lord, it is the other way around: the assent of the Son of God has been with the Father from all eternity because the Son has been of one will with the Father from all eternity. When he sends the Son on his mission, the Father therefore has no need to wait for his assent. It is as a *man* that the Son gives his assent *after* receiving his mission. The works he does are done within the Father's divine will, which is at the same time his own divine will. If he were to do them as mere man, they would be no more than an attempt. He would then *attempt* to do the will of God. His achievement would be eternally inchoate, and he would have to renew his assent constantly throughout his mission. He would have to test and question himself whether he was still within his mission. He would have to offer himself to God ever anew and receive ever anew from God the assurance of being at this moment still at the heart of his mission without deviation. But since Christ is God in human form, the mission and its fulfillment are one. There is no break or interval between the Father's command and its accomplishment by the Son. No hesitation, no reflection or taking counsel, no possible difference of opinion exists in their work together. (We are here not talking of the Lord's suffering and temptation, for in these mysteries the Lord freely assumes the *human* situation. But this, too, is done within the divine mission and is contained in it.) The Son takes his obedience to the Father with him into this earthly life so completely that he lives on earth solely from the perfect unity of will between Father and Son. His obedience is the obedience of a God. And yet, as such, it also is the model of what the perfect obedience of a man to God *could* be. If he were not also this model, if his obedience did not have this human dimension but were purely divine, it would, so to say, have nothing to do with us. It would forever remain the inner mystery between Father and Son, inaccessible to human words and thought. But as obedience of the Lord in the flesh, it becomes for us the perfect example. It is an obedience as human as it is divine: in the severest tests of temptation and Passion, it is the human in Christ that is tested, not the divine; and it is the man who obeys at the cost of a strength totally failing. The obedience of the incarnate God is equally divine and human in every other work he does. Divine in its outward manifestation, its active performance; human in its interior attitude, in the availability in which he is open to God, in everything that calls for receptivity, particularly in his temptation and suffering. He actively works his miracles, which are divine; but he never works a miracle in his human receptivity, for example, the miracle not to feel the suffering, the temptation in the desert, not to be sensitive to hunger and thirst, or to come down from the Cross, etc. He is receptive as man, active as God. Because his works are first of all divine and only as such the unattainable model of any human action, he can say, "*The works which I am doing*". Of merely human works he would have to say, "The works which I try to do". There is here another contrast between the Lord and us: while the Lord is divine in his works, human in his suffering, in our case the divine is seen when we are passively receptive, the human in our active mediation. When we are enabled to mediate the divine, it is already refracted and weakened. It is easier and more spontaneous for us to receive the divine action than to mediate it. In passing through us, the divine has, first of all, to overcome our sin, or at least our inclination to sin, and suffers in this the loss of some of its power. But in passing through the Son, the divine is strengthened through his perfect purity. That is why his works bear witness to him. They do not lose their color, are not weakened or refracted. They are the pure works of the Father. One recognizes at once that they are the Father's works and that the one who works them at his command is the Father's perfect representative: the Father has granted him to do the Father's works and equally to do them as his own works.

5:37. *And the Father who sent me has himself borne witness to me. His voice you have never heard, his form you have never seen.*

The Father's works always bear witness to both, Father and Son: they are the Father's works even *though* and also *because* it is the Son who carries them out. If he were not the Son, he would not be able to do these works, which bear witness to the unity of the one who commissions them with the one who carries them out. It is precisely this unity on which the Jews are missing out. For this unity, which is the meaning and the heart of all the works of the Lord and which allows us to see and hear the form and voice of the Father in the Son, is understood by man only when he attains to his own unity in faith. This is explained in the following words.

5:38. *And you do not have his word abiding in you, for you do not believe him whom he has sent.*

The Jews possess the Father's testimony in the Son, but they have not heard his voice or seen his form because they do not believe. The unity of the mission and its accomplishment has its foundation in God, in the unity of the Trinity, but can be recognized by man in the unity of faith, love, and hope. Apart from the Son, no one has seen the Father or heard his voice. But if a man sees the Son with the eyes of faith, which reveal to him who the Son is, and if he hears the Son with the ears of faith, which enable him to hear the divine voice of the Son, he can also recognize the Father in the Son, see his form and face and hear his voice. A man should not ask where this hearing and seeing begin. He will experience their beginning and end, their manifestation and coming to life as soon as he surrenders in faith to the Son and accepts his word. The seeing and hearing of the divine form and voice are totally linked to faith, are a function of this faith, possible, however, only in love. For love opens our eyes and our ears. And the love that makes contact with the Son becomes immediately and in itself faith. The Son would not value a love that does not lead to faith; only faith legitimates any love for him. Whatever else may pose as love for Christ could be anything, but not love.

As believers, men will hear and see, and the Father's Word will remain with them, the Word that was in the beginning and through whom all things were made, the Word that includes faith, hope, and love, the Word coming from the Father and going back to the Father. In such a faith, the Word of God remains *abiding*. This abiding is anything but stagnant lifelessness, much less rigidity. Nothing is more alive and alert than this abiding of the Word of God in the believer. Once it has been properly heard, it will awaken faith and begin to work outside itself. It can remain abiding only by being at work and by being passed on to others. This does not mean that it is sown out and gathered in as harvest, for often enough it will be different people who do the sowing and the gathering. Yet the sowing is fruitful even though the harvest cannot be seen; as soon as the Word of God falls into the good soil of faith, it will grow and increase, in the believer as much as in his surroundings. The abiding of the Word is its transformation into a spring that ever increases its flow, giving itself and spreading all around. That is why the mystery of faith is so close to the Eucharist. Here, too, the lifeless dry piece of bread is transformed into a living and infinite grain through the ritual word of the priest. This transformation takes place for the sake of faith, unto faith, and through faith. Not the personal faith of the priest is meant, but the faith of the Church, the substance of faith itself, which the Lord gives to the Church and which yet *abides* in him. The Consecration at Mass is the gift of the Lord's love to faith. It could be compared to a guarantee certificate that can only be filled in with the believer's name, is valid only for him, and receives its value only through his signature. There exists as little connection between the piece of bread and the Lord's Body as between a coupon and the goods for which it stands. The connection for the believer is made solely through the Lord's freedom. In the Host, his love for the Father and for men becomes concrete for those who believe: he gives official power over himself to an individual, but for the sake of the whole community and for love of the Father: in order to lead all through faith to the vision of the Father.

As soon as a person believes in the Son, the barrier between this life and eternity is removed, the dividing line between sinners and saints becomes blurred, no separation remains between the Father and man, for the Son is everywhere making the connection as Mediator. A believer will find it impossible to hear the Word as only word without allowing it to become life-giving in himself and around him. Thus, the distinction between action and contemplation will also disappear. Everything becomes one in the love for the Father, for this love will finally be only surrender to and movement toward him. It includes everything the believer is and does, everything God is and all he has created. This ultimate limitless love bears the name *Christian faith*. This is the last completion, the fulfillment of what God planned when he created man and when he made the New Covenant out of the Old. This fulfillment is not a distant Utopian possibility but an immediate and urgent quest bearing the possibility of fulfillment in itself.

The eyes and ears of faith are therefore made so keen by God that they see and hear *everything*. They are no longer bound to human limits and possibilities. The grace of God has stretched them into the infinite. Human seeing and hearing are in themselves limited: light can become too bright for the eye, sound too loud for the ear. But as soon as faith becomes real faith, as soon as the Son is truly accepted, all human limitations fall away. The life beyond does not begin *behind* the curtain of human sight; it consists in seeing the face of God and hearing his voice through all earthly and human reality, through the incarnate Lord, through the saints, the neighbor, through the world itself. The grace God gives in faith is a grace that meets and recognizes the grace of God everywhere. Only if there is (or might be) in the world absolute, unlimited sin in a man, no transparency to God remains (or would remain). But as soon as there is a mere beginning of grace or openness to grace, then the believer's grace of mission links up with this real or possible grace, increases it, and becomes a channel for it to God. Wherever in a man there is still a space left for grace beside the sin, and wherever a believer has the mission to look after this person and turn him to God, there also the person's sin is through this grace made visible to him; for him, light is thrown on its details and contours, so that in this light the sinner may be helped to free himself from it. He learns more from God, who enlightens him, about the sinner than from the sinner's words. In this sense also, the believer's sight and hearing have been enlarged so that one grace unites with another grace through him. What takes place is a kind of Eucharist of grace, not in the sense of distribution, but in the sense of reuniting with the Lord. The life of faith in different people has the characteristic of uniting and flowing together in the Lord and—as faith and love, passing through the Lord—in the unity of the Father. For faith comes ultimately from the Father and keeps the inclination of returning to the Father, always with the Son, taking the believer along.

5:39–40. *You search the Scriptures, because you think that in them you have eternal life; and it is they that bear witness to me; yet you refuse to come to me that you may have life.*

The Jews seek eternal life in their Scriptures; therefore, they seek God and his Son in them. Yet they are seeking, not in faith, but with their minds already made up. What they are seeking is to serve themselves; it must have the meaning they are expecting, and they are so full of their own expectation that no room is left for the expectation of God. They would like to tell God what he is to say to them. The eternal life they strive for so much would fundamentally be their eternal death. What they imagine eternal life to be is nothing but the eternal duration of themselves, of their present earthly life. They refuse to see that life on earth can be only the prelude and foreshadowing of their eternal life. They seek eternal life as prolongation of their own desires and ideas and do not understand that they ought to be doing the opposite to find it: lead their earthly life according to God's plan, or better: allow him to mold it by his love. Their main task should be meditation in which to lay themselves open to God in order to let him alone act and then—as best they can—cooperate with him in his work. Their actions should follow on and continue God's action, not the other way around. Their work should be allowing him to work in them, not by being passive, but by offering themselves without words, in silent surrender. But that is difficult for them. They would like to underline the meaning of their own actions with words and explanations, to prevent being misunderstood. Ultimately, they are only full of themselves and blind for the divine Scriptures.

The Scriptures bear witness to the Lord. The Old Testament offers some intuition of his qualities and predicts him. And even though he has not yet appeared in the flesh, he is already present in the Father and in the Father's revelation. Everything points to him, moves toward him. Following the direction in which the Scriptures point, the Jews ought to reach him. There they would find life. It is the Lord who takes care of the eternal life, not man himself. That is why he asks only faith, not a self-chosen and self-seeking deed of our own. The meaning of human life does not correspond to our own projection. It must be the meaning the Lord gives it. All this is visible already in the Old Covenant. At the great moments of grace, God's love becomes visible to such an extent that grace can hardly be understood apart from the Father's love for the Son. The night of separation of the Father from the Son has not yet been endured, so the Son as such cannot yet be seen but only divined. But in this premonition, the link between Father and Son, insofar as it is absolute love, becomes clear.

5:41. *I do not receive glory from men.*

The Lord does not need a human testimony to receive his perfect glory. He himself is the Father's glory, and nothing of this glory comes from men. His objective glory cannot be affected in any way by the positive or negative testimony of men. They may and should bear witness to him and find him glorious. But that does not constitute his glory, and if they refuse him their recognition, his glory is not diminished. His glory is the glory of God; it is absolute glory, not dependent on anything else. It is not tied to human frailty, to the flesh, to loneliness, to the battle against sin and its conquest. It rests in himself but is always on the increase because it witnesses to the love of the Son for the Father and of the Father for the Son, who renders him constant and ever-increasing glory, glory that is nothing less than the unfathomable expression of the trinitarian life.

5:42. *But I know that you have not the love of God within you.*

The Lord cannot explain or show them the glory he possesses in God. This would require that they possess the love of God. Without this love, they cannot understand anything of God. As long as they do not love God, love him absolutely, it is impossible for them to comprehend the absolute character of the love and the glory of the Son or this Sonship itself. And since they do not comprehend his Sonship as divine, neither can they comprehend that he can be the Son of Man. The Lord knows that they do not have this love, for if they had, they would be in him (and he would know them as such) and would have eternal life in him, sharing in the love between him and the Father. He knows them as not being in him; he does not find them in himself, though there is a space for them. He sorely pines for their presence in this space; he feels it as a painful emptiness. And not for him alone is this empty place painful; in the bosom of triune love itself, the participation of the Father's creation is painfully missed.

5:43. *I have come in my Father's name, and you do not receive me; if another comes in his own name, him you will receive.*

Only one who does not come in his own name can bring the fullness of love. He bears it more fully in himself when he does not come in his own name; then he has room for what he loves. But men do not accept the Lord precisely because he comes in the Father's name and not in his own and, so, without the prerequisites that men expect from other men. They imagined that the Son, when he came, would come in the well-known form of a man, with personal qualities, a clearly defined character, and a destiny easy to comprehend and to read. His "virtues" could then serve as a model; one could grow up to him and imitate him. Or else he would come as God and be so different from them in appearance that he could be easily recognized and specified. In either case, they expect someone greater than themselves but to whom they could directly relate in every way: as either a perfect man, clothed in every virtue but without mystery in his relationship with God and thus easily summed up by them, or as God clothed in the mystery of the Divinity, which would remain inaccessible to them. They would then have bowed down before this divine power, of which they know it must be adored, and in this dutiful adoration its demands on them would be satisfied. For the rest, the Mosaic law would have remained in force. Only one thing would have been new: they would have felt enriched by knowing that another prophecy had been fulfilled. This God of their dreams would have had to be surrounded with splendor, enabling them to celebrate the glorious festivals as they know and love them, with magnificence and the sumptuousness of humanly experienced glory.

But now God faces them with this infinite, incalculable problem of this Son, who is a man like others but who shares all the time a mystery with God. This mystery enfolds not only his Incarnation, of which they know that it is enveloped in mystery, but also his abiding and continuing Sonship all through his earthly journey, where he remains mysteriously united to the Father in a communion that is unfathomable to them, and finally in the mystery of the Trinity itself. They would have expected that the Son, speaking of and showing them his intimacy with the Father, also would have entered into intimacy with them, so that they could gain a somewhat exhaustive insight into both intimacies. They had imagined it to be something objective, open to investigation.

However he might have appeared, as man or as God, he certainly would have had to be a superman embodying every virtue and also the moral recipe for them to achieve a similar perfection. They are very much aware of the fact that in their own lives sin remains a constantly recurring obstacle and that this is the sin of their flesh. They find plenty of excuses for this presence of sin, even while knowing that their interior is in a wholly disordered state.

They see their drives as an expression of the power of evil and concupiscence, stronger than themselves, so that they cannot remedy the situation. It is the sin of the flesh in the wider sense of the word, and in every form, that they cannot master. Their expectation was that they would be asked to overcome these drives and become perfect men. Their bodies should find the power and possibility to tame them. They would like to see in the Lord a perfection that would allow them to see clearly the signs of a battle won and the virtue resulting from it. They also imagine that every fault and sin would have its own moral treatment and method for overcoming it. They know that there are drives that are good and right in their origin; they are sinful or enticing to sin only when they are exaggerated and satisfied wrongly. The Lord as perfect man would have to possess vast possibilities in overcoming every temptation and conquering it. In other words, their ideal is one of a constant ethical battle. Their surprise is all the greater now that they do not see in the Lord the least sign of a moral battle, no shadow of self-renunciation, not the least inkling of sin. They imagined they could read him like a moral code, a collection of precepts. But he says nothing about any moral struggle. His sole answer to all their questions is always the same; he asks only one thing: faith and love. He points in only one direction: to the Father. The secret of the holiness he demands consists in loving the Son and doing the Father's will out of this love. This sole answer is for him the starting point for every other exposition of his Commandment; their personal struggle, their personal sin and its remedy, their growth to perfection: all this is included in this single sentence and subordinated to it. They expected praise for every fault they might overcome, that they would get rid of their sins one after the other, and in between there would be a resting point, a review, a pause. Their dream of perfection was a step-by-step ascent. But now that the whole of perfection is placed in love, the goal can no longer be defined, neither the final one nor the intermediate ones. The goal has become infinite; it is absolute perfection, and the way to get there (there is a way) knows of no steps, no gradual progression, no brisk advance, but at most a blind stumbling forward without clear overview. It is clear that the goal cannot be reached as far as man is concerned; death will find him still on the way; everything will remain unfinished. Only God can transform the pilgrimage into arrival. But we are not spared any trouble; we have to carry on almost without hope, and hope is justified only where it is cherished together with the two others, faith and love, and is one with them in complete unity.

This puts an end to their highest expectations. So the human appearance of the Son of God is for them an immeasurable disappointment. Their concept of progress is shattered against his simple demand. They would like to be able to combat their individual faults with adequate means and methods—less stealing, less lying, less coveting—and mark some progress in this way. But it is clear that this kind of progress, which measures and compares, would not bring them the smallest step nearer to God according to the mind of the Son. They would only succumb to another far worse sin: self-righteousness. Their entire progress would take place in sin; its measure would be sin: more or less sin. They can only see this everywhere. They measure the positive by its distance from the negative. They look at the negative to measure the positive. But the Lord demands that we look only at him and not at sin at all, nor at ourselves. They think the occasions of sin should be increasingly avoided, that one could learn to keep well clear of them. But the Lord leaves his own in the midst of the world and does not spare them rubbing up against evil and temptation. He does not take temptations or their drives away. He leaves all this to them because it is necessary; they need to feel and know themselves as sinners in order to find their sole God and Redeemer in him. In him and in him alone they ought to turn away from the world and toward the Father. He will be their way only in this kind of conversion. But his opponents do not want such a way. The Lord brings what he has received from the Father: faith, love, hope. They are looking for a method of morality. Faith, love, hope cannot be measured against sin, give no human handle to progress. They cannot be measured at all.

If another were to come in his own name, they would receive him. He would come in the name of his own perfection. He would bring a teaching and a method, an instruction how to overcome one's drives and sins with one's own strength, through oneself. They would have been impressed by this because it is within their own horizon. Intention and success could be seen and read in each case. Judging and measuring, which is what men prefer to do, would come into their own, would have their day. Someone coming in his own name would be like a book that can be read page after page, by acquiring one new concept after another. One reader would be on page two, another on page seven; they could discuss it and instruct each other; it would be interesting and also harmless. The meaning of it all would be convincing and be logically linked together. It would be a religious and ethical system, and they would joyfully accept it. One could turn to other things from time to time and after an interval continue again where one left off. The lessons already learned could be quickly refreshed to avoid the danger of building on unsure ground. But in the Lord's "system" no general view is offered, for its essence is love. Here everything is infinite; everything is made relative to love; nothing can be deduced; love always comes first.

5:44. *How can you believe, who receive glory from one another and do not seek the glory that comes from the only God?*

They want to learn from each other in the sense of theoretical knowledge and comprehension. In this game, which they play among themselves, religion and morality also have their place. It remains on the human level and expresses in appearance and form human behavior. In *this* human form, God is comprehensible to them, and the man transparent. They want to remain on *this* kind of human level, covered against every surprise. They do not accept responsibilities that are not quite clear to them. If they are to believe, it must be in such a way that their faith will rest on circumstances known and understood by them. Therefore, it is not the glory that comes from God that they seek. They seek the glory that is found on the human level. And this is the reason why they cannot believe. They would have to seek God alone, to surrender and lose the lead, give themselves over to the divine, in such a faith. Perfection, which is conformity with God's views, consists in this surrender to God in faith and in love.

5:45. *Do not think that I shall accuse you to the Father; it is Moses who accuses you, on whom you set your hope.*

The Lord will not accuse them. If he did so, they would begin again to measure and to judge, to examine how far they have been judged rightly and how far with injustice. They would not recognize the love that is the only thing he proclaims. So he does not give them an occasion of sinning against love. Their accuser is Moses, the Old Covenant in which they are rooted. This Old Covenant is full of the Lord; it is as a whole nothing but the promise of the Lord. They seek him in this promise and do not find him because he has come to fulfill it. Neither can they see that by ignoring the Son, they force Moses to accuse them before the Father. Moses is responsible for the true interpretation of the law. The Lord points this out in order to shake them up on their way, using their own ideas and arguments to make an impact on them. He bypasses himself and his law of love; he withdraws to the standpoint of the Old Covenant. From there they can be proved to be already in error. There they are already in the wrong.

5:46. *If you believed Moses, you would believe me, for he wrote of me.*

Their faith is selective and arbitrary already according to Old Testament standards. They want to believe only parts of revelation because they are ever busy justifying themselves. They assert their right to explanations and accept only what is intelligible to their reason. Their human journey must begin and continue with themselves and from themselves. In all seriousness, they believe in their own action more than in the love of God, in their own judgment rather than in God's judgment. They see themselves in the center. Their measure is their own love, not the ever-greater love of the Lord. They cannot bear the comparative with the infinite, into which the Lord's love places them, because they have no overall view of it. Increase is wanted only within a limited field where the goal can be reached. What is more must never be an ever more. There must come a point where they can say that they have arrived. This makes them enemies not only of Christ but also of the Old Covenant, in which Moses already demanded pure faith, pure surrender to God's guidance and law. Moses was in contact with God; he was open for the mystery, the cloud, the darkness, for what is ever greater in God. Every word he wrote bears witness to this openness. If the Lord had appeared to Moses, Moses would have believed at once; if the Jews were to stand today where Moses stood, their faith would have remained in movement and open to life; as people who were looking out for him, they would have recognized him as the one so long awaited. A believing Jew is in the most favorable disposition for becoming a believing Christian.

5:47. *But if you do not believe his writings, how will you believe my words?*

For them, the law of Moses is pure letter. Since it is the written word, they accept it as an unchanging and, so, limited and clearly defined document. It has for them the strength of a protocol sealed once forever. There are no surprises in it; everything is fundamentally clear and defined. Its interpretation resembles that of a scientific text or a historical theme. The Scriptures are for them the exact image of that ideal of perfection that they imagine the Messiah to embody, and themselves in his following. Both fit together as the interior to the exterior. Both are totally lifeless. What is alive in the letter of Moses is its pointing forward to Christ, the lead it gives to faith. But that does not interest them. In rejecting Moses, they have already rejected Christ himself and can believe him even less when he proclaims the law of life and love, freed from the letter. They do not want to be carried away into this eternal movement of life where man can become ever more enlarged to the infinite, because the Lord is forevermore the Ever-Greater.